DATE			

Embarrassment In Everyday Life

-

What To Do About It!

by

Edward Gross, Ph.D.

An ETC Publication

Library of Congress Cataloging-in-Publication Data

Gross, Edward
    Embarrassment in everyday life: what to do about it / Edward
Gross. — 1st ed.
      p.   cm.
      Includes bibliographical references and index.
      ISBN 0-88280-122-8: $23.95
      1. Embarrassment.   I. Title
BF575.E53G76   1994
152.4—dc20   93-42672
                                                CIP

Published by ETC Publications
      700 East Vereda Sur
      Palm Springs, CA 92262-4816

In memory of

Gregory P. Stone (1921-1981)

For colleagueship and fellowship

CONTENTS

Embarrassment in Everday Life

What to Do About It

HOW THIS BOOK CAME TO BE

"Man is the only creature who blushes, or needs to"

The saying is usually attributed to Mark Twain. This book is my answer to why humans have that need. However, my studies of embarrassment began not merely with general interest but with a personal experience.

As a university professor in the early 1960's, I discovered we had an administrator who was a plain embarrassment to everyone. We used to hesitate to look at the morning newspaper for fear there would be some new report of a gaffe or blooper he had made the day before.

Then the university leaders did an amazing thing. Instead of removing him, they appointed a committee to "advise" him. Actually, the committee really ran his division for him while trying to keep him from doing anything silly.

In surprise I asked the chair of the committee why the university did not simply remove or transfer him. "Oh no, " he answered, " We could never do that. That would be too embarrassing."

Embarrassing! "To whom?" I asked. He answered, "To the people who had chosen him in the first place. To the staff around him who had projected the illusion that he was making sound decisions. To the public relations staff of the university who had to assure everyone in the community that the university has sound management."

To prevent all that from happening, the administrator kept pulling down a very high salary while the other faculty who had their own jobs to do had to spend their time doing his job for him.

That incident so impressed me with the power of embarrassment that I decided to look closely at it as a research subject. I began a serious inquiry into embarrassment with a colleague, Gregory P. Stone. Together we worked out some of the basic theory of embarrassment. We found few research studies in sociology. There were plenty of anecdotal reports, books of bloopers and jokes but few serious studies.

Therefore we decided to gather our own material. We first solicited what we called "specimens" from students at the university in beginning and advanced classes as well as from more mature persons. We received around 1000 such specimens. We published a serious paper on our early findings. Greg and I continued to work on that material for a while. Then I left that university to come to another one and our collaboration came to an end.

I went on to research in other subjects (I am a specialist in the study of organizations such as businesses, government bureaus, hospitals, and universities). I later wrote a second article on embarrassment by public figures which generated considerable interest as well as mail. As time went on, I began to gather reports from newspapers and magazines. In the late 1970's, I again began to solicit specimens. Students remained a good source but as I did my research on organizations both in the United States as well as in other countries (mainly Australia, Israel, Canada and Great Britain) I would seek examples or simply observe them in government offices, factories, business offices and homes for the aged.

As word of my interest got out, I was the subject of an article in PEOPLE magazine and appeared on the Johnny Carson and other talk shows. Those experiences led to more unsolicited examples of embarrassment. Altogether I guess there were another 1000 or more that came in that way. Recently in response to some newspaper interviews, more specimens came in by mail or over the telephone.

In analyzing the specimens, the procedure was first to check on whether it was new or simply a version of one already received. Then would come categorizing the specimen and regrouping categories into broad types. Often I would excerpt a phrase or portion for later quotation if the excerpt seemed appropriate. Many of these appear in this book after modification (if necessary) to prevent identification.

In case you are one of those who provided a specimen or letter, rest assured that I have been careful to preserve confidentiality by destroying the letter or report after categorization. Embarrassments, by definition, are personal.

In sum this book represents my conclusions from work over the last 30 years (though not continuously of course) I have written several scholarly sociological books and a great many, journal articles. But I would not be honest if I did not admit that I have written this one because it is so much fun. I hope you find it fun and perhaps learn from it as well.

Finally, a word to my sociology colleagues. Although the whole book is written in a spirit of fun, I am serious about the analysis and I hope it stimulates research. The specimens are no sample in any sense but a basis for trying to make sense of embarrassment as a human social activity.

Are all the embarrassments reported to me genuine? Some persons ha‿ asked me that and I can only reply that I do not know. A few seem so unlikely that I wonder. If the doubts are strong, I have not used the report. But human behavior is so full of unlikely events that it takes a certain amount of arrogance to toss anything out. I can only testify to those I have witnessed myself. On the other hand, where an incident is reported with details that could not be fabricated, then there seems little doubt.

Still, I do not really worry about the truth-falsity issue. Even perfectly true stories often come to us embellished, and some stories are so poorly told that even when true do not sound believable. There are even stories drawn from fictional work that we know to be made up but which are such wonderful tales that they are worth quoting for the human truth of character they reveal.

In the end, such revelation is what we are after. What does getting embarrassed tell us about human character? When we find that out, then we may understand why humans go so far as to make up stories about getting embarrassed. If, as Mark Twain (perhaps) said, only humans have a need to get embarrassed, then we had better start taking embarrassment seriously. Further, since it is the serious things in life that provide the most fun, we should not be surprised if we start laughing, even if we do so only to keep from crying.

ACKNOWLEDGMENT

To: ELSPETH

Editor, Proof Reader and
Everything Else

ABOUT THE AUTHOR

Edward Gross has a Ph. D. in sociology from the University of Chicago and a law degree (J.D.) from the University of Washington. He received two Fulbright awards for research as well as numerous professional invitations to deal with sociological issues and labor problems. He is the author of seven books as well as many scholarly articles and is listed in WHO'S WHO IN AMERICA.

He has been a professor for over 30 years at various universities both in the United States and abroad. He states that besides the rewards and satisfactions of being a teacher, watching and studying embarrassment has added a spice of its own to those years.

PART I

Understanding Embarrassment

What can we do about embarrassment?

To answer, we need to recognize five basics:

1. Embarrassment is part of being human.

2. Embarrassment is not trivial but can cause damage which may even be devastating.

3. Yet despite such damage, embarrassment turns out to be beneficial, even essential to life.

4. Research has uncovered the causes of embarrassment: why and when it happens. With that knowledge, we can see how to deal with it.

5. Shyness and shame must be distinguished from embarrassment. Seeing how shows us the special tactics that work best.

These five basics make up the first five chapters.

Chapter 1

Embarrassing Moments— They Happen to Everyone

"Embarrassment! What a strange thing to write about!" That is what a friend of mine said when he heard I was planning to write this book. "Everybody has had embarrassing things happen. Can you do anything about them? That's what I'd like to know," he asked.

It is easy to understand my friend's puzzlement. Why write a whole book on embarrassment? I am going to consider such things as: tripping, slips of the tongue, getting someone's name wrong, walking into the wrong room, dropping a dish, discovering your clothes are torn. What strikes you is how perfectly ordinary and how universal such experiences are. If so, what is so terrible about them. They make us blush, apologize, and feeling the blush, become even more embarrassed because we're blushing? Why should such universal experiences make us embarrassed at all?

My search for an explanation led me to an answer to the question my friend asked. After all, embarrassments make you feel uncomfortable. Sometimes you feel awful, leading you to say things like: "I could have died." Can anything be done? My answer is yes. Often they can be prevented or hidden. When they cannot, what you can do is control them so that the suffering and unpleasantness is eliminated, or at least reduced to a minimum.

Discoveries in social science can offer help, and it is the kind of help you can apply yourself. What do we know about embarrassment?

EMBARRASSMENT IS UNIVERSAL

Although it's more common at some times than others, people seem to get embarrassed in every society and always have. Writing in the 4th century B. C., the Chinese philosopher Mencius tells of how his mother had to remind him to be careful to avoid embarrassing persons when he might be"at fault" (presumably in private) by raising his voice and, at a minimum, lowering his eyes. Anthropologists' records of tribal practices leave no doubt that embarrassment is ever-present.

Forms vary but the basic feeling is there. There is a rise in temperature, increased heart rate and muscle tension. Many peoples laugh, lower their heads and avert their gaze, as we do, but with variation. Several studies report very little gaze aversion among Greeks, Italians and Spaniards, but a great deal among residents of the United Kingdom. Residents of South China stick out their tongues to signal a boo-boo. The Balinese cover a fear of *faux pas* with elaborate polite rituals.

Some tribal peoples suffered new sources of embarrassment when Europeans invaded their traditional homelands. Women in the South Seas, for example, felt quite fully clad in their dark skins until missionaries made them put on loincloths and bras. They then began to try to cover themselves with their hands, or rushed away like frightened gazelles when anyone looked at them, feeling that the loincloths and bras drew indecent attention to what was modestly unemphasized before. In Japan, the concept of "face" assumed almost sacred proportions. In historic times, men and women would commit suicide rather than suffer the humiliation of loss of face. It is important even in present-day Japan.

When William the Conqueror first stepped ashore in England, in the 11th Century, it is reported that he slipped and fell forward into the mud upon his two hands. His fellow chieftains were at first alarmed, seeing the event as an evil omen. William, recognizing it as no more than a slight embarrassment, lifted up his hands with the mud on, saying:

> See, my lords, by the splendor of God, I have taken possession of England with both my hands. It is now mine, and what is mine is yours.

A neat recovery! The story may be doubtful since it is also told of other military heroes but it does suggest that embarrassments have been common throughout history. Even the Bible opens with a story of a couple who were, at first, not ashamed, nor embarrassed by their nakedness. Things soon changed, and have never been the same since.

EMBARRASSMENT COMES AT ALL AGES

Parents have written to me that they have seen signs of embarrassment in their children as early as 3 years of age. According to one study, about half of children age 5 show embarrassment. After that age, it shows up in practically all children, even the blind who have never seen a blush, as well as children with other defects.

If children do not do anything embarrassing, they soon become embarrassed by their parents. Isabelle Leeds, a special assistant to a former Governor of New York, recalls a time when her most fervent wish was that New York's Waldorf-Astoria Hotel would disappear.

> I'm tone deaf but my father wouldn't believe it. He thought I was a musical genius and he got his dear friend, who was musical director of the Starlight Roof, to listen to me play the piano. When we got there, there were still guests in the room. But my father's friend had agreed to hear me play, so he sat me down and I played. You know that old saying about "They all laughed when he sat down at the piano." That was me. The audience was silent, perhaps in shock. The musical director was kind. "Your daughter should get married," he said, "I'm sure she will be a wonderful mother."

She did become a mother, and has, according to *New York Times* columnist Enid Nemy, (from whom we have the above story), lived an interesting, glamorous life, but still cannot put that experience out of her mind. Other children continue to smart from the pains of being introduced to their fathers' friends as "chips off the old block," or of having their accomplishments paraded before visitors. I still feel a slight blush as I recall my mother's insistence to movie-house cashiers that I was "only 10" years old, when, already pushing 12, I should have been paying "junior" admission prices.

It gets worse with teen-agers. They change so rapidly in body, in understanding, in relations with the opposite sex and in the beginnings of serious thoughts about a career. They seem to be constantly red-faced with embarrassment. The boy who was always told how cute he looked when he got angry now finds his parents warned by his teacher that they had better get some counseling for him in a hurry. The girl who had always been "a bit tall for her age" now discovers that she is taller than most of the boys in the room and they are giving her the wrong kind of

14

attention. Adolescents are at a stage where they are continually being evaluated by teachers, parents, career counselors, peers and the opposite sex. As a consequence, one of the most common kinds of embarrassment they experience is mere exposure, as illustrated in the following example, from a sophomore high school student:

> My most embarrassing moment in the last two weeks was when I went to class late the other day. Everyone looked up and I couldn't even think to give the teacher my excuse for being late but went right to my seat. She had to ask me for my excuse and I had to walk up in front with it. When it was all over I sure was relieved.

These experiences don't sound like much, but they can be devastating when you're a teen-ager.

As you get older, you overcome some of these problems only to be met with new ones. Psychologist Jerome M. Sattler found college students to be more concerned with interpersonal relations, such as forgetting names, speaking mistakes and being embarrassed for others. After leaving college, embarrassments are found to cluster around money (such as being caught with not enough), having one's competency questioned and on matters of personal responsibility. New jobs and new careers present new challenges and new embarrassments. The following example was supplied to me by a doctor:

> When I was a student intern in a hospital, the professor used to train a group of us by taking us with him on his rounds. We would come up to a patient and we would be asked to examine the patient and make recommendations.
> Suddenly the professor turned to me, and said: "Dr. Jones, will you examine the patient please?" I was so excited that as I seized my stethoscope, I somehow pulled off the

rubber tip on the end, which then fell to the floor and rolled under the bed. I dropped to my knees and began reaching around under the bed looking for it. The next thing I heard was the voice of the professor, saying in rather weary tones to the patient:

"While Dr. Jones is under the bed, another doctor will examine you." I often wonder what the patient thought was going on.

EVEN THE HIGH AND MIGHTY DO NOT ESCAPE

Most of us can take some comfort from the fact that high status doesn't enable persons to escape the perils of embarrassment. When the U. S. Supreme Court ordered then President Nixon to surrender his secret Watergate tapes, the task of writing a first draft of that opinion fell to the Chief Justice, Warren Burger. According to famed Watergate investigator Bob Woodward (writing with Scott Armstrong):

> The Chief's (Burger's) drafts of the first sections of the Nixon-tapes opinion invited anarchy. The Court had fractionalized. In addition to the objections everyone had noted, the Chief's work was sloppy and ungrammatical . . . (Justice) Stewart agreed. The Chief was, once again, not doing his homework. (Justice) Brennan criticized the Chief's work—its general imprecision, its aimless rhetoric, its lack of analysis. . . The Chief, Brennan declared, was going to embarrass the Court.

The final opinion was actually a composite put together by the entire court.

Others are not so fortunate to have someone who can save them. Take the case of a football player named Roy Riegels,

16

playing for California (Berkeley) in the Rose Bowl. Before thousands of fans, he seized the ball and, dodging all possible tacklers, neatly ran almost all the way toward the wrong end zone. As well as handing a victory to Georgia Tech, the opposing team, this feat earned for him the name of "Wrong-Way Riegels." If there is a Hall of Fame for blunders, his name will be there.

We need not assume that embarrassments are peculiar to the U. S. Willy Brandt, former Chancellor of West Germany and winner of the Nobel Peace Prize in 1971, found himself in an embarrassing position in 1980 when word got out that, though married, he was living with a press officer of his Social Democratic Party, who was about to give birth to their child. It was pointed out that he had been trying to get a divorce from his wife (his second, and the mother of his three grown sons) but had been stymied by community property differences. Although such occurrences are not uncommon these days, neither Mr. Brandt nor his children were particularly pleased to become the subjects of editorial comment.

Our own government can hardly claim any superiority over others when it comes to embarrassment. Former President George Bush, out to show the Japanese that we are serious in improving economic relations, proceeded to vomit on the Japanese prime minister. This appears to be an historical first in relations between heads of state.

Outside of politics, business and other organizations have their share of embarrassments. Firestone rubber has had to recall damage us tires. Lockheed officers found it difficult to explain payments to foreign government for favored considerations of their airplanes. Ford designed its Pinto with it gas tank in such a position as to endanger occupants. Japanese and German car manufacturers are being forced to recall several models because of defects. Clark M. Clifford, trusted advisor to U. S. presidents from Harry Truman to Jimmie Carter, found himself defending his role in a sordid bank scandal in which his bank was used as a front for foreign corruption or worse. At a more everyday level, hospital maternity wards occasionally mix up babies, and universities are found to have frauds on their faculties including a celebrated case of a man with no formal qualifications who was on the teaching staff of a major medical college.

Such public embarrassments involve more than particular persons. Those responsible not only embarrass themselves, they embarrass the government or the company. We can't help but wonder what it can mean that the Ford Motor Company, a name practically synonymous with the automobile industry, allows a car, the Pinto, to be manufactured when it may actually threaten people's lives.

Even trying to illustrate such dangers can lead to worse embarrassment as happened when NBC News tried to show what could happen to certain General Motors trucks. The trucks were equipped with what were said to be defective fuel tank assemblies. NBC News agents apparently (the facts are not clear) arranged for explosives to be used in a simulated crash to make sure the potential danger (the car bursting into flames) would really occur in front of the waiting cameras. The head of NBC News, who may have been innocent of direct involvement, was forced to resign anyhow. But not all embarrassments are so sad.

EMBARRASSMENTS CAN BE TRIVIAL OR IMPORTANT

Embarrassments vary in their effects, some being good for a laugh, others leading to a good cry or worse. Here is a report from Victoria, British Columbia, Canada:

18

Murphy's Law states that if something can go wrong, it will. It did for a Victoria woman who called police recently to report a man in her bed. It seems her boyfriend was lying in her Murphy bed—the kind that folds up into the wall when not in use—when something went wrong, a police spokesman said.

Slam. Up went the bed. Up went the startled boyfriend. Upside down with his head stuck in the assembly, the boyfriend was unable to budge the bed. Neither could the young woman.

Police responded to the call and finally freed the embarrassed young man.

In another case, a woman writes to a newspaper columnist, Judith Martin (who speaks in the name of a "Miss Manners" on matters of etiquette). She asks whether her husband was correct in laughing at an incident that occurred at a lavish, formal Bostonian party.

At the party, a lady in a low-cut gown tripped, stumbled, lurched across a table falling face first into a bowl of guacamole dip, and in the process "popped out" of her top. After an initial stunned silence, practically everyone in the room burst out laughing, even though it was obvious that the lady was terribly embarrassed. Then the hostess rushed over to help her and ushered her upstairs.

The writer asks whether the laughter was not bad manners and inconsiderate. Her husband argued that he and others meant no harm.

"Miss Manners" replies that she is rather skeptical that such a thing actually happened. She says that ignoring the incident as if the woman had merely trailed her sleeve in the dip would

19

imply that you hadn't noticed. That would suggest that the lady did that sort of thing frequently and her friends had gotten used to it. Though Miss Manners does not approve of the laughter, she can understand. She suggests waiting till later to share other hilarious, embarrassing incidents in sympathy with the woman.

Both the Murphy bed and guacamole incidents can be dismissed as funny anecdotes. They are not funny to those people to whom they happen. At the time, as the expression goes, people want to run and hide, or just "die."

So much more the case is true for embarrassments that can have more serious consequences. Some of these are not innocent. People can be reduced to tears by embarrassing insults that they cannot handle. Sometimes people will deliberately embarrass others as a punishment. This will happen when some persons are making false claims and others feel the need to puncture their balloon and cut them down to size.

Businesses are confronted by the problem of what to do with persons who are no longer productive, but once were. To fire them would not only be embarrassing as well as humiliating to the individuals, but would also be a bad signal to the younger people. Some of them might well think that they do not want to associate themselves with a firm that treats those that have given their lives to it so callously. So companies will soften the blow by "kicking a person upstairs," or creating positions as "senior advisor," as the British have done in the imaginative rank of "field marshal" for its old soldiers who refuse to fade away.

We need not look far for embarrassments which have hurt companies, or even brought down governments. We still have Watergate fresh in our minds. Earlier generations experienced the Teapot Dome scandal which involved a secretary of the interior as well as an attorney-general, who used their positions for personal gain. The British government was nearly brought down in 1962 by the indiscretions of its Minister of War, Profumo. He was finally punished, not for his indiscretions with the famous Christine Keeler, but for his lying about it. The British are remarkably tolerant of human frailties. A boldfaced lie on the floor of the Commons is simply going too far. When Profumo resigned, he offered reassurance there had been no breach of security. Then what was he concerned about? He put it in these words:

> I cannot tell you of my deep remorse for the embarrass-
> ment I have caused to you (the prime minister), to my col-
> leagues in the Government, to my constituents and to the party
> which I have served for the past 25 years.

Nor are embarrassments confined to persons in high places in government. Sport historians and older baseball fans can hardly forget the 1919 World Series when it turned out that the Chicago White Sox, heavily favored, had agreed to lose so that gamblers could take advantage of the odds to bet on Cleveland, the opposing team. There was embarrassment for everyone. These included the players who did it, the managers that let it happen, the gamblers who were finally exposed, the officials who could not see it when it took place before their trained eyes, the fans who were badly let down, and not least the Cleveland team, who soon realized if the series had been thrown, that meant they had not won on their own merits. Here embarrassment spreads out like ripples from a stone dropped into a pond engulfing everyone.

21

RECOVERIES FROM EMBARRASSMENT ARE RARE

From time to time we read of famous recoveries, clever or snappy returns which seem to rescue a lucky few from their embarrassments. Queen Victoria was once entertaining the Empress of Japan at a state dinner. Midway in the meal, fingerbowls were brought, and the Empress, not knowing what they were for, assumed they were for drinking. As soon as she lifted hers to her mouth, Queen Victoria immediately lifted hers to drink. Of course, then everyone followed suit. The Queen's gesture was meant to prevent any embarrassment to her guest. One wonders whether the Empress returned to Japan with stories of how the British seemed to be partial to a very thin, tasteless soup.

A story is told of Beatrice Lillie, the comedian, who was once giving an interview in her Park Avenue apartment. It was a warm summer's day. The doors to her balcony being open, suddenly a pigeon flew in and perched on a lamp top. Miss Lillie looked up, paused, then said: "What, no messages?"

The theatre has many such bon-mots and recoveries. On one occasion, Leo Slezak, a famous Wagnerian tenor, was performing in the opera Lohengrin. The part calls for him to be drawn onto the stage in a boat pulled by an enchanted swan. As American actor, Walter Slezak, Leo's son, tells the story, a stage hand got the wrong cue and sent the swan and boat off onto the stage, leaving Leo standing there. Leo looked around for a moment, then called out quietly to nearby stage hands: "What time's the next swan?"

Another recovery is credited to the former Senator Margaret Chase Smith, for a long time the only woman senator in the U. S. Senate. At the time when Eisenhower was still president, she was asked whether she was considering running for the presidency.

She shook her head vehemently, denying any interest in the office. But the reporter prodded her further.

> "Think about it for a moment, Senator," he said, "Have you ever thought about what it would be like to wake up in the morning and find yourself in the White House?" Senator Chase paused, then said: "If that happened, I would apologize immediately to Mrs. Eisenhower and go straight home."

Such recoveries are not only rare but for every successful one, there are attempted rescues which make things worse. A New Zealand newspaper reported that a certain man was a "defective in the police force." In a later edition, the editors expressed regret for the error saying the sentence should, of course have read that he was a "detective in the police farce." Elsewhere, an obituary reported the death of a "bottle-scarred" veteran. Later, after deep apologies, the editors said it was obvious that they meant to say that he was, as everyone knew, "battle-scared." There are times when nothing goes right.

HOW, THEN, SHOULD WE GO ABOUT DEALING WITH EMBARRASSMENT?

The point so far has been to show how common embarrassment is, and how everyone, high and low, faces it. We cannot simply wish it out of existence, and it is much too widespread and devastating to ignore. What can be done?

First: We must come to an understanding of how embarrassment works. What is there about it that makes it so upsetting? That is the subject of the next chapter, Chapter 2.

Second: We will then make a surprising discovery. Embarrassment is actually a good thing. Without it, we could probably not survive. That is so unexpected that I give a whole chapter to it, Chapter 3.

Third: We get into the heart of the beast. In Chapters 4 and 5 we will see what causes embarrassment, and how it differs from shame and shyness.

As we take these steps, you will find that embarrassment is something you can handle. It will still happen to you but, as you come to understand it better, you will begin to see that there are ways of taming the beast. Then we will get into specific strategies and tools for managing embarrassment.

Chapter 2

Why is Embarrassment
So Upsetting?

Most people think of embarrassment as a common but usually trivial thing. Those of us who are middle-aged smile at the teen-agers' problems: a boy's getting tongue-tied in asking a girl a question, or a girl's cry that she "would rather die" than let him see her dressed in "this old thing!" On the other hand, teen-agers wonder what can lead some middle-aged grownups to be so uptight about having to wear just the right dress, or what the neighbors think about their lawn. Can we simply dismiss embarrassments as persons sometimes ask us to do? Can we take comfort from the pronouncements of our neighborhood philosopher who reminds us that in 100 years, what difference will it make?

In 100 years it *won't* make any difference to us. Nothing else will either. But 100 years from now, I predict that people will still be getting embarrassed at much the same things that trouble us. Why should that be? That is the question I want to consider now. If the president of a country gets upset because a member of his government does something that embarrasses the whole country in the eyes of the world, that is understandable. But why should we also get upset about the little things like stumbling as we walk, about make-up that runs, about knocking over a styrofoam coffee cup? It turns out that such happenings, big or little, have important consequences. They interrupt what is going on. They can smudge or even destroy an identity and they can lead to our being intimidated when we should not be. Such consequences are important.

INTERRUPTION

When persons get embarrassed, they are momentarily stopped. While they hesitate or hunt desperately for something to do, whatever was going on is aborted. Suppose something exciting has happened to Alice that she is telling it to her friend Lorne. Suddenly, she says to Lorne:

> You'll never believe what came next, Mike. I looked up and there in front of me was the strangest sight...

In her excitement, Alice has been carried away and called her friend Lorne, "Mike." What happens then? We do not have to guess. I have several actual cases documenting the ending. Here's one (with name changed).

> Lorne is reporting:

> When she got my name wrong like that, I wrinkled my brow because I was puzzled. How come she called me by another name? What was she thinking of? Was she even aware who she was talking to? Then, since I was wondering about those things, I wasn't paying attention to what she was saying. So I lost the point of her story. When she finally stopped, and asked me what I thought, you know what I said? "How come you called me Mike?"

The person telling the story began to blush, apologized, and tried to make up for it. But the whole conversation has been sadly wasted. You can probably recall such experiences from your own life.

Conversations make up much of our everyday life, and they can be embarrassing in many ways. A person you are talking to may look away, then suddenly apologize. A person can embarrass you by looking so intently into your eyes, and hanging on your every word and gesture that you become self-conscious and lose your train of thought. Other conversations are embarrassed by people standing too close to one another, or too far apart. Sometimes people throw us when they have a slight blemish, say, a wart in the middle of their nose. We try desperately not to embarrass the other by looking everywhere else except at the wart, our very efforts revealing our discomfort. It is no small matter to talk with someone and make it work well, for any false move embarrasses us. It affects our attention, and can mean that the message does not get through or we create the wrong impression.

Much of our life consists of cooperative movements (and conversation is cooperative) sometimes of greater consequence. On one occasion the Minnesota Orchestra was having a three-week music festival, featuring a brilliant young Russian pianist, Aleksander Slobodyanik. He was playing the Mozart Piano Concerto No. 15 but things did not go well. He apparently suffered a memory lapse in the first movement and substituted for Mozart some inventions of his own, leaving the conductor desperately trying to discover where the pianist was. According to *Minneapolis Tribune* critic Michael Anthony, Slobodyanik did recover but the rest of the performance seemed to be spoiled.

27

Anthony wrote:

One of Mozart's grandest, most spirited concertos was given an introverted, cramped, murky reading by the pianist, who, apparently had been unnerved by the whole thing.

That musical example reminds me of a personal experience when I performed as a supernumerary in the opera *Aida*. A "super" is a nonsinging role (in fact the director had to warn several of us who would get carried away and hum along with the chorus to kindly shut up) but this opera calls for lots of supers. There is a great triumphal march when the hero comes back from the war, and directors like to have hundreds of supers marching across the stage in time to the glorious music. To create this effect, you march across, leave the stage, change your costume quickly, then fall into line and march across again, so giving an impression of vast armies on the stage.

In choosing roles, the director decided that I should carry the hero's battle standard, leading the army onto the stage. I began to quake in fear, telling the director: "Oh no, don't put me out in front. You see, without my glasses, I am practically blind. I will lead the army straight into the orchestra pit." "Don't worry," he reassured me, "you'll have no trouble."

I soon saw why he was so self-assured. The hero was followed on stage by 4 horses (directors love horses, some even going for elephants or camels), and I, of course, was right behind the horses. Horses doing what they do when they get nervous, I had no trouble following behind. I could have done it blindfolded. Unfortunately, the mess left by the horses distracted the audience so much, they could hardly restrain their laughter. So the triumphal scene lost much of its glamor.

That experience was fun (though not to the director who had strong words with the horse-trainers who were supposed to have "processed" the horses ahead of time) but sometimes even important international negotiations can be interrupted by embarrassing events.

In June of 1980, then French President, Valery Giscard d'Estaing, surprised everybody by suddenly flying to Warsaw for a conference with Soviet President Leonid Brezhnev, seeking to persuade Russia to withdraw from Afghanistan. Unfortunately, he did not take the trouble to inform his Western allies, the U. S. and Germany, of what he was up to. Those countries had been *privately* meeting with the Russians, seeking to do the same thing as Giscard, but hadn't gotten anywhere. Now here was Giscard seeking to show up their failure as mere ineptitude. As it turned out, Giscard too failed, providing the Paris daily *Le Monde* with the opportunity to observe in a cynical editorial:

> Brezhnev got what he wanted. The Soviet press will present (Giscard's) presence in Warsaw as a sign of the end of the quarantine in which the Kremlin's leadership has been locked for five months since the rape of Afghanistan.

In the end, both Germany and the U. S. had to accept the whole thing as an embarrassment to their claim that there was such a thing as "Western consensus" on how to handle the Russian invasion, and Giscard himself was laughed at as practicing "Lone Ranger diplomacy." That embarrassment contributed to his defeat in the subsequent French elections.

In this way, embarrassment can interrupt something important that must go on. A surgeon told me of an operation:

Everything was going fine until the intern that was assisting me handed me a tool that was all wrong for the purpose. I couldn't believe it, at first, so I stared at it, then at him. Then I got angry and threw the tool down onto the tiled floor, where it clattered as it bounced around.

Everyone looked up, and the intern began to sweat with embarrassment. I felt he should. Anyone that could make as bad a mistake as that was either untrained, or just not paying attention. In either case he shouldn't be there. The intern suddenly turned around and left. I later had a long talk with him. It turned out he was worried about some personal matters which was really no excuse. He should never have tried to carry on.

While this little drama was going on in the operating room, the operation itself came to a halt. The nurses stopped paying attention to what they were doing, other assistants turned away to watch the tool on the floor and students who had been watching the operation now were watching the embarrassment itself! Meanwhile, the patient was lying there, luckily not knowing that everything was on hold. When people get embarrassed, they are "out of play," at least for a moment. They cannot carry on, and have to stop to recover their poise. Others who become conscious of this embarrassment feel embarrassed for them, and they go "out of play" too, so bringing whatever has been going on to a halt. Embarrassment stops the action.

IDENTITY DESTRUCTION

French President Giscard provides an example of what can happen to a person's identity when he becomes embarrassed.

Here he is, seeking to play the dashing international hero when instead he is shown to have played into Moscow's hands. We need not limit ourselves to the great and celebrated. Each of us, however humble our role, also has an identity that we must protect. A left fielder who drops an easy catch will be embarrassed, whether he is in the major leagues or the bush leagues. It would be worse in the bush leagues since such persons are being watched for signs of promise, whereas a major leaguer may be excused as simply having an off day.

Especially difficult are those who are trying to create a credible identity, such as ex-convicts or ex-mental patients. Robert Edgerton, an anthropologist who has made a special study of the mentally retarded, points out that when such a person is released from a mental hospital, he faces the problem of accounting for that year or so that he was in the hospital. If these persons are borderline normal (as is usually the case for those who are released), they are often quite aware of the low opinion that "normals" have of them. They have (before hospitalization) often been called "dummy" or worse and it hurts. They are therefore anxious not to have anyone know where they have spent the last year and are quite careful to avoid potentially embarrassing incidents. Yet the missing year in their biography will come up whenever they apply for a job, see a doctor, even have a casual conversation.

To cope with this problem, a few chance open admission that they were in hospital. They claim it was an error or that they were in for treatment of "nerves." An ingenious preventive of embarrassment was described by one person. He went to a rummage sale where he bought an old photograph album full of family pictures. He then "adopted" that family as his own. He explained that he had spent the year visiting some of those pictured in the album.

31

Some of the funniest embarrassments can have sad outcomes. A woman whose husband had served on the staff of a United States foreign aid program told of a diplomatic reception in which she found herself seated next to a foreigner. He sat stiffly, every inch the diplomat in his dark gray suit, with perfectly matched conservative tie and black patent leather shoes. At last, after a long silence in which no one stopped by the couch he stood up to leave only to notice that his fly was open. He quickly sat down, and in hurriedly trying to zip up unnoticed, caught both ends of his tie in his zipper.

He tried to shoo his hostess away when she offered help but in raising his head, he only tightened the tie around his neck. He slowly began to turn blue. By the time the hostess returned with a pair of scissors, everyone in the room was focused on the unhappy diplomat. In his hurry to escape, he snipped the tie in half and ran out of the room, the long ribbons of his tie waving from his fly.

Unfortunately, his troubles were far from over. Within hours everyone in the diplomatic community had heard of the incident and relayed it to friends elsewhere. When persons met him, their eyes would drift down uncontrollably to his famous fly. He had become a figure of fun, his reputation as a serious diplomat destroyed. His country had to call him back to a bureaucratic job where he'd not be noticed and the incident forgotten. I doubt if people did ever forget. The woman who told me about it certainly hadn't. At least for a time, perhaps years, his identity had been utterly destroyed. His embarrassment was not funny to him. And for the rest of us our identity is always precious to the point where any assault on it is not funny to us either.

INTIMIDATION

If embarrassment can interrupt essential activities, and if it can discredit or destroy someone's identity, then we have good reason expect that people will do everything they can to avoid it. It isn't just that it's unpleasant but rather that the consequences can be so serious. But people may go too far in seeking to avoid it to the point that they may be intimidated or frightened into silence and acquiescence when they should act.

There are fewer more frightening experiences than that of being trapped in a burning hotel. It was not surprising that someone should write to Dear Abby, seeking advice on what to do should a hotel guest *suspect* a possible fire. She advises calling the fire department *yourself* before alerting the hotel operator. In explanation for this action she quotes Captain Richard H. Kauffman of the Los Angeles County Fire Department:

> Believe it or not, most hotels will not call the fire department until they verify whether or not there really is a fire, and have tried to put it out themselves. Should a guest call to report a fire, the hotel will almost always send a bellhop, security guard or anyone else who's not busy to investigate. Hotels are reluctant to "disturb" their guests. Fire engines in the street are quite embarrassing and tend to draw crowds.

Fire Captain Kauffman then goes on to urge hotel guests to call the fire department themselves. He grants that the "hotel may be a little upset" but, says he, "who gives a damn?... you may have saved many lives."

His claim that fire engines "are quite embarrassing" is really extraordinary. They are of course, if there is no fire. But there is

33

clearly another embarrassment which will prevent people from acting as he advises. Most hotel guests are reluctant to make a fuss, or unnecessarily alarm other guests. Worst of all, what if there is no fire? Most guests cringe at the thought of having to face a not surprisingly irate hotel manager and have to explain why they took this drastic action. The fear of embarrassing others and being embarrassed combine to make it unlikely that anyone will really call the fire department.

We often think that we are blasé and liberal about sexual matters. A study by Canadian professor of family studies Edward S. Herold of a sample of 19 year old women who had experienced sexual intercourse and were currently involved in a relationship reported that these women confessed to a lot of embarrassment when they had to ask for different forms of contraception. Embarrassment was higher when they had to seek contraceptives from doctors or pharmacies near their parents' homes and especially high when getting condoms.

Nor can we dismiss such a finding as peculiar to women. A recent national survey of males aged 20 to 39 by the respected Alan Guttmacher Institute reported that 27% of the men said they were embarrassed to buy condoms. Although we cannot be sure that such embarrassment prevented use of condoms, embarrassment research suggests that such prevention probably occurred in many cases. Since the survey was carried out in part because of a desire to encourage condom use to prevent HIV and AIDS infections, we see the dangers that fear of embarrassment can lead to.

That fear can hurt all of us when it stops persons from offering help when we need it. One study showed that persons would not offer help if the situation was ambiguous. They were concerned that the person in trouble might actually not need help with the result that the helper would end up looking foolish. A study by British psychologist Robert J. Edelmann and associates found that subjects were quite willing to help a shopper pick up a dropped packet of tea but much less willing if it was a box of Tampax tampons—too embarrassing.

Then there is the problem of not getting involved. You'd think persons would help most those who need it most. But one study showed persons were *less* willing to help a person with an apparent injury (his arm in a sling and his knee in a brace) than one without injury. Others found it too embarrassing to help persons with a disfiguring stigma, such as a large red birthmark than more attractive persons. Psychologists Dianne M. Tice and Roy F. Baumeister presented experimental subjects with what looked like an emergency—a person apparently choking on a doughnut. Then they waited to see who would interrupt the experiment to seek help. The subjects had been tested for "masculinity" (the traditional stereotype of assertiveness, decisiveness, stoicism in the face of danger). To the surprise of the experimenters, the more masculine the subjects, the less likely were they to offer help. They felt apparently that their masculinity would be threatened should they embarrass themselves by doing something inappropriate or stupid. This study tells you that when you need help, don't look to the he-man types.

There is a lot of evidence that persons needing help or social services from a government bureaucracy are often inhibited even in seeking what is rightfully theirs. They fear the embarrassment of being put down or being treated as inferior. Especially tragic is the discovery that many persons delay or even avoid medical examinations because of being too embarrassed by the examination itself. A recent report found a particular reluctance to undergo a rectal examination, particularly those over 65 who are at the highest risk for developing colorectal cancer . Some of the unwillingness is certainly the unpleasantness of the test itself, even the simple stool test. A part of the problem is brought out in the slogan used by the American Cancer Society: "Don't die of embarrassment."

Some classic studies show how intimidating embarrassment can be. Social psychologist Solomon E. Asch asked persons simply to judge which of three lines of different length was the shortest. The differences were very large and there was no question which was the shortest. When the person was asked to do this in the company of 6 or 7 others (all of whom were paid confederates of the experimenter), and when all of the confederates chose the *longest* line, a high proportion of the subjects were willing to go along with the group, against the clear evidence of their own senses. Although Asch did not specifically investigate the cause, there seemed little question that many felt too embarrassed to contradict the will of the majority.

In still another famous experiment on obedience, carried out by psychologist Stanley Milgram, subjects were willing to administer electric shocks of clearly dangerous levels when asked to by the scientists conducting the experiment. They continued to do this rather than face the embarrassment of defying the experimenter. One piece of evidence that embarrassment was operating was what happened when the experimenter issued his orders by telephone rather than in person. We know that embarrassment is greater when someone is physically present than when the onlooker is at a distance or invisible. When the experimenter issues his orders by phone, nearly three times as many subjects found the courage to disobey.

The desire to enjoy the approval of our fellows leads to the desire not to appear foolish or stupid. This desire can be so strong that it will lead persons to do things they do not wish to or are ashamed to do. A striking political case is provided in an autobiographical report of George Orwell. He tells of a time

36

when he was a British official in Burma. An elephant had got loose, killed one man, but had quietened down and was feeding himself in a public market. He was not dangerous, unless approached. Orwell would have preferred to leave him alone until his caretaker could be found, but felt he had no choice. He wrote:

> ... suddenly I realized that I should have to shoot the elephant after all... A sahib has got to act like a sahib; he has got to appear resolute, to know his own mind and do things. To come all that way, rifle in hand, with two thousand people marching at my heels and then to trail feebly away, having done nothing—no, that was impossible. The crowd would laugh at me. And my whole life, every white man's life in the East, was one long struggle not to be laughed at.

Orwell does shoot the elephant and concludes his report by saying:

> I often wondered whether any of the others grasped that I had done it solely to avoid looking a fool.

What a political statement! Here is a British official, a representative of the most powerful nation on earth at the time saying he was a mere pawn in the hands of the natives. The whole structure of British authority depended on not being laughed at. Yet there is a basic truth in his claim. Authority does depend on its being taken seriously. Once people in authority act in an embarrassed manner then their self-confidence starts to erode, and they begin not to be taken seriously.

There is yet another way in which embarrassment is related to authority. Many persons continue to exact obedience or even respect because no one wants to appear stupid by challenging them.

The most common occurs at public speeches when someone with established credentials proceeds to describe the complexities of the tax structure, the reasons why heating oil prices have gone up or why crime refused to come down. In many cases, as you can recall from your experience, the chairperson calls for questions. There are few, and then the chairperson meekly suggests that "apparently our speaker answered all the questions." Yet as we walk away from such meetings, there is often a flurry of questions, which we address to each other: "Why didn't he take into account...?" "Maybe he's right, but that's not the way it is out where I live," and so forth. Few risk the embarrassment of directly challenging the speaker, with the result that the speaker is allowed to prevail, or at least appears to. He retains his position. What would happen if more persons could somehow overcome their fear of embarrassment and begin systematically to challenge those in positions of authority? But overcoming fear of embarrassment is no small thing.

HOW ABOUT GETTING RID OF EMBARRASSMENT?

Since embarrassment interrupts important events, discredits our identities and intimidates us, why should we put up with it? Besides, it's painful and makes people laugh at us. So maybe we should design a campaign or a therapeutic program to simply get rid of it.

It turns out that embarrassment is like any other painful experience. It points to some problem, just as physical pain may be a symptom of disease. To get rid of pain provides temporary relief but to try to get rid of pain altogether would destroy the body's major way of alerting us to need for action.

So too embarrassment provides us very powerful benefits, some so great that we would not want to get rid of it even if we could. Benefits? Yes, as we'll see next.

Chapter 3

The Hidden Blessings
of Embarrassment

Embarrassment a blessing? It usually doesn't feel that way. How is that possible? I don't mean the feeling is a blessing—we all know that it hurts. Later on I'm going to deal with how we can reduce that hurt. But what we need to understand now is that the ability to get embarrassed does us a lot of good. It acts as an alert system which helped us to survive in times past and still helps us. It exposes fraudulent claims. Finally, it is a major aid to children and teenagers in the process of growing up and learning how to cope with the world.

EMBARRASSMENT AS AN ALERT SYSTEM

Think of what happens when we get embarrassed. We hesitate, tremble, blush, stutter, or perspire. Our voice may quaver or fail us altogether. Sometimes we close our eyes, cover our face with our hands, or appeal meekly to others for help. Inside our bodies there are further sensations. We get queasy in the stomach, feel wobbly or dazed, or even suffer such a loss of balance as to almost fall over.

Such a mass of symptoms cannot be dismissed as trivial. It is this involvement of the whole body that makes me feel sure that there is something very basic about embarrassment.

Perhaps it has been programmed into our gene pool. I would say that embarrassment is one of the great human emotions, having as much evolutionary significance as fear, anger, or aggression. Many, if not most cases of embarrassment occur when we are shown up as incompetent or unable to handle some problem that we should be able to handle. Those situations are threatening to us or may create problems when others are depending on us to perform.

What does the human body do when faced with a threatening situation? Because of our animal makeup, we are programmed to respond in ways that worked well in prehistoric times when we were faced with threats, such as possible attack from another animal or human.

The actual biological processes are not well known, but sociobiologist Desmond Morris gives us a plausible account. Our bodies are mobilized for action through the autonomic nervous system. That system gives signals for the release of adrenaline and other hormones into the bloodstream. The heart beats faster and blood is drawn away from places where it is not needed (digestive system, bladder) to where it is needed, such as the lungs for extra oxygen and the muscles for quick action. There may be extra blood flow to the brain as well, though that is not so clear, and probably to the face, which is covered with tiny capillaries, as well as to the eyes which may bulge the better to focus on the danger.

All of this is most useful if you must act by attacking or by running away. If you do act, then all the energy that has been mobilized is now drained off and if you were successful, you will feel relieved and even pleased with yourself.

But what if you are confronted with an embarrassing situation, with one in which you do not know what to do? Consider this case:

I was part of a panel on day care facilities for working mothers . . . I was all geared up but my heart was pounding. I felt hot and started to sweat. I was breathing so hard I could hardly talk . . . I barely heard the chairperson introducing me and then I thanked her calling her by the wrong name! I wished I could drop through the floor and just die.

Embarrassments are precisely those situations where we are all set to act so our nervous system gets us all hyped up. Then we are suddenly stopped by the embarrassment, but the body is mobilized to keep going. The resulting frustration and all that pent up energy with no place to go makes us feel upset and wobbly with indecision. Out of the urge to do something, we may even do something stupid, apologize and then wish we could just die.

WHAT'S THE POINT OF EMBARRASSMENT?

So much activity, we may be sure, is hardly random. What it all comes down to is a punishment for not being ready, for venturing into a situation which one cannot handle. Should a monkey baby, for example, wander a short distance from its mother, it may catch the eye of a predator who is looking for a juicy morsel which is too weak to protect itself. The monkey's mother may then, if she gets the chance, rush over and yank the infant by the tail even at some danger to herself from the predator. The infant learns that it has ventured too far. So too, the unpleasant experience of embarrassment is a natural warning sign. It is as if "Nature," if it could speak, were saying:

You have ventured into a situation you could not handle. By doing it you endanger yourself, and all the others who are

43

depending on you. See to it that it does not happen again. To make the warning vivid, it is going to hurt.

It is my contention that the ability to get embarrassed proved a valuable aid in enabling our ancestors to survive. Those who did get embarrassed were more careful in avoiding vulnerable situations, and so survived to pass on their genes to others. Those others then inherited the same ability to get embarrassed.

BLUSHING

The great Charles Darwin, author of the theory of evolution, was himself puzzled by embarrassment. In his classic work on *The Expression of the Emotions in Man and Animals*, he devotes a whole chapter to the subject of "blushing." Of course many animals "blush" in those areas of their skins that are not covered with hair. But such blushing seems only evident as a sign of rage or of sexual excitement. Blushing with embarrassment seems, Darwin says, ". . . the most peculiar and most human of all expressions." He goes on to point out that you cannot bring on an embarrassed blush by direct stimulation:

> We can cause laughing by tickling the skin, weeping or frowning by a blow, trembling from the fear of pain, and so forth; but we cannot cause a blush . . . by any physical means— that is, by any action on the body. It is the mind which must be affected.

But there's more to it. Although Darwin called attention to blushing, he didn't think it had any function. He dismissed it as no more than a by-product of self attention. Researchers since

44

Darwin have tried to find out why such a strong reaction should have persisted in humans if it really has no function.

It is not easy to study blushing. Dermatologists tell us that facial warmth and reddening can result from central control centers in the brain, from the brainstem, and from sources that affect the small capillaries in the face and elsewhere. The hot flashes of menopause seem to originate in the hypothalamus but the circulation of blood at the skin surface seems to have a different source than the flow to the brain. Other conditions such as Reynaud's disease and migraine can also affect circulation. So can alcohol, exercise, and spicy food, as we know from our own experience. There are even chronic blushers who, according to British researcher Robert J. Edelmann, say they blush in any situation involving people and who find they are simply unable to cope with their blushing.

Those few researchers who have managed to separate out blushing find that persons practically never report blushing when they are alone. The blush is usually immediate (within two seconds in one study) and lasts for up to 15 minutes. Blushing appears quite involuntary, as Darwin noted. People can't bring it on or stop it by any act of will. People are intensely aware of it and of those who witness it. For instance, psychologists Mark R. Leary and Sarah Meadows report that their subjects (220 undergraduate students) said they were especially likely to blush when they've been caught doing something improper or shameful and when they've looked stupid or incompetent in front of others.

What Blushing Says

Italian researchers Cristiano Castelfranchi and Isabella Poggi have come up with what I think is the most likely function of blushing. Since it is so visible, it is clearly a signal that something's wrong. As they put it:

> Those who are blushing are somehow saying that they know, care about, and fear others' evaluations and that they share those values deeply; they also communicate their sorrow over any possible faults or inadequacies on their part, thus performing an acknowledgment, a confession, and an apology aimed at inhibiting others' aggression or avoiding social ostracism.

In brief, the one who blushes is telling us he knows he's goofed, he knows we know he has, he is asking forgiveness, and begging to be excused and be invited back into the community of those who know how to behave. What is more, since embarrassment is something he can't put on, we are further assured that he is sincere in his promise to do better if only we will accept him.

But what about Blacks, others of dark skin or those with large beards covering much of the face (as was true of our remote male ancestors)? For Blacks (and presumably others), Castelfranchi and Poggi answer that, even if no one else can see it clearly, *they* at least know it by the rise in temperature, and the unpleasant feelings of embarrassment. They are thus informed by their own bodies that they have done something wrong, that others will disapprove or are disapproving and that they should smarten up and try to repair any damage. So it is at least, for them, a learning device.

Even for such persons, they are not left only to blushing. All of us do more than blush. We avert our eyes and hang our heads, which biologist Eibl-Eibesfeldt tells us, many animals also engage in as gestures of appeasement to other animals. So even those whose blush is not easily visible will be betrayed by their eye and head movements.

Blushing and other accompaniments of embarrassment turn out to be appeasement signals. A dog (and other animals) will, when threatened by a larger or dangerous dog, suddenly roll over on his back and expose his soft, vulnerable belly, as if to say: "I am no threat to you. You can even hurt me and I won't resist." So too, embarrassment gestures seem to have the same function, an appeasement gesture to others for what we have done.

Since appeasement among animals does act to save their lives or prevent injury, it clearly has evolutionary significance. Those animals that developed that ability genetically were more likely to survive and so pass on the genes for appeasement to their offspring. Those that didn't aren't around any more.

With humans (and here we can only speculate), those who developed genetically the ability to blush when violating group norms and values communicated their guilt and willingness to change. They would then more likely be forgiven, allowed to carry on and so pass on their genes to the next generation.

We can be very glad we get embarrassed. It even looks good, especially in the young. Don't we all get some pleasure in seeing someone blush? We can hardly stop smiling, or even calling it to their attention which then makes them blush even more! We accept and forgive those who are willing to admit their mistakes. A mistake is what a blush reveals. Embarrassment is a giant involuntary alert system that has powerful survival value since it forces us to attend to what went wrong and to think quickly about repairing the damage or making sure it doesn't happen again.

That's not all. Embarrassment has other values.

A KEY TO SURVIVAL IN A WORLD OF
STRANGERS AND CON MEN

Whatever the evolutionary significance embarrassment may have had in our remote prehistory, research shows it to be of major importance in the industrialized world of today. The archeological evidence is that humans once lived in small bands, in which everyone knew everyone else, and was probably related to many of the others in the band as well. But the coming of the great agricultural revolution in the Neolithic Period—the cultivation of cereals and the abandonment of a nomadic way of life— as well as the domestication of animals led soon to the increase in population and growth of cities. This heralded the historical world of great civilizations.

We have been growing ever since, now reaching such levels as to lead population experts to express concern about the sheer carrying capacity of the earth. To feed this rapidly growing army of hungry mouths, the services of modern industrial productivity and agricultural innovations have been drafted. The self-sufficient farm, feeding its own inhabitants, is rapidly disappearing into history, however important it may be as a nostalgic symbol. The pouring of displaced persons into the cities has brought about an employee society.

Over 90% of employed persons in the United States now work for others. Close to 60% of those in the private sector work in large organizations with at least 100 employees, and that does not even include the 1 in 7 who work for government. This concentration in large organizations is experienced by children when they start school and pursues them through high school

48

and university, many of which are very large. Our correctional institutions, hospitals, churches, unions and voluntary associations also can be very large.

What all this means is that persons increasingly find themselves, whether inside organizations, or on the street, in the company of strangers. When these are persons from whom we seek help or professional assistance, we may be taken in by frauds or those with false credentials. Often an embarrassing disclosure may tip us off that a person is not what he seems.

SHOWING UP PRETENDERS

In a collection of blunders culled from many sources, Bill Bryson, Jr. writes of a doctor in Salzburg, Austria whose cakebaking skills aroused the suspicion of a patient. It turned out he had no medical credentials but was a pastry chef. In another case, a Greek was practicing medicine in Rome when a Greek patient examined the document on his wall which others had assumed was a medical diploma. The patient found it to be document from the merchant marine.

In many kinds of work, inexperienced recruits may try to pass themselves off as old hands. They study manuals or practice and memorize technical terms. But what they can't hide are their embarrassments at sudden revelations of their ignorance of "tricks of the trade." These are the knacks and skills that can only by learned on the job.

For example, a study of firemen reported that experienced firemen avoid looking up when scaling a ladder lest burning material fall on their face. A man who does look up frequently gives himself away as a beginner and may easily get hurt as well.

Sociologist Jonathan Rubinstein found that rookie policemen can be spotted by their wearing of a standard necktie rather than a clip-on. A dangerous criminal would choke the policeman

49

by grabbing his necktie. The clip-on simply comes off in the criminal's hands.

Such embarrassing failures on the part of would-be deceivers are enough to show them up but some persons go much further. They manufacture additional incriminating evidence to do themselves in.

Such was the case with a newspaperwoman for the *Washington Post* who wrote a story about an 8-year old heroin addict, leading to her earning a Pulitzer Prize. But the mayor and police could not find the boy, and neither could the *Post* itself when they tried.

That might have been the end of it but the reporter proved to be her own undoing.

In her resume submitted to the *Post* when she applied for the job, she claimed a B. A. from Vassar, an M. A. from the University of Toledo plus fluency in several languages. To the Pulitzer Prize people, she felt the need to embellish that record a little by adding a year of study at the Sorbonne University in France, plus a couple of more languages. These discrepancies soon became public knowledge, especially when the Toledo newspaper for which she had worked expressed some puzzlement. It turned out she had spent only 1 year at Vassar, but she did have a B. A. (not an M. A.) from the University of Toledo. The cracks in her credibility now widened into crevaces, leading Ben Bradlee, executive editor of the *Post* to demand a full checking out of the story.

The Pulitzer Prize was withdrawn and given to the runner-up, leading to the reporter's resignation with apologies "to my newspaper, my profession, the Pulitzer board, and all seekers of the truth." There was enough embarrassment for everyone to share, not only for the reporter herself, but for the *Post*, which published an editorial entitled "We Apologize," plus a 12,000 word report on the episode dealing with "why it all happened." This newspaper, the site of the famed Woodward-Bernstein Watergate story, perhaps the most important piece of investigative reporting in recent history, was itself shown to have done its share of "stonewalling,"

In a world of small communities where we know each other, we can depend on other people to be what they seem to be. We know them well enough to know how much trust we can place in them. But when we meet strangers, we need some guide to help us. The person who tries to pretend he is something different from what he is runs the risk of committing a boo-boo or worse. That will reveal him for what he is.

GROWING UP COOL

I have been told that occasionally a candidate for an executive position will be suddenly presented with the need to make a splitsecond decision on what is claimed to be an emergency situation. The candidate is then judged not only on the prudence and wisdom of the decision but also on his ability to control his emotions, think rationally under stressful conditions, and not be embarrassed by having to perform in front of others. Those are rare abilities but especially important for persons in positions of responsibility.

How do we develop those abilities?

The ability to control yourself in situations which might be embarrassing is not limited just to those in positions of responsibility. We would all like to be able to brazen our way through gaffes, slips, or "bricks," as the British call them. Among the most common are "spoonerisms" in which we transpose the initial letter of sounds of words. The Reverend W. A. Spooner, sometime warden of New College, Oxford, who gave us the name also gave us some of its best examples. Preparing to offer a toast to Queen Victoria, he said: "Let us drink to the queer old Dean." He also castigated an undergraduate because he had "tasted two whole worms," and had "hissed all my mystery lectures."

An equally embarrassing form of speech is the malapropism which confuses not initial letters or sounds, but similar words. Mrs. Malaprop in Sheridan's play *The Rivals*, must deal with Lydia Languish who is as "headstrong as an allegory on the banks of the Nile." Speaking of education, she avows that "geometry" is useful that one "might know something of the contagious countries." Spelling too, should be studied so that one be "able correctly to reprehend the true meaning of words." These kinds of embarrassment seem to be universal and since there is no way of undoing them once they are said, what we might hope for is the ability not to be thrown, apologize and simply get on with it.

The value of aplomb or poise seems so obvious that you might wonder if it can be taught. It *is* taught, as a part of growing up. Small children tease one another, push one another off balance, and challenge each other to games of poise such as Follow the Leader, or in later years, arm wrestling, "outstaring" each other, or word games calling for quickness and the ability to recover. Such games are found among persons of all ages, especially among adolescents.

Kids As Teachers

In England, Iona and Peter Opie have collected vast quantities of material on the lore and language of school children. Many of their examples relate to what persons find embarrassing in later life and teach the skills needed to avoid it. Any undesirable feature of clothing is immediately commented on. For

52

example, if a boy's cap is twisted to one side, he is asked: Are you wearing that cap, or just walking under it?" The need to maintain proper limb discipline in concealing underclothes is underlined by:

> I see London, I see France
> I see someone's underpants.

A fart is greeted by:

> I'm a kid, you're a goat
> You smell, and I don't.

Smoothness in speech is emphasized. In response to someone who says, "Well . . .," another will say:

> What's the good of a well without water.

And the user of too many "eh?"s is advised:

> Buy straw, it's cheaper.

The values of independence are driven home by scores of taunts of cry-babies, whereas one who threatens to go home and "tell mother" is mocked:

> Tell her, smell her
> Kick her down the cellar.

There is even a special set of games called "embarrassers" by the Opie's. These are basically tricks to corner a person and catch him or her in an embarrassment. One is told a story of a donkey trapped in a field by high walls and other barriers, and is asked how he got out. After every reply is denied (e.g. the wall was too high to jump over), the person gives up and says:

I don't know.

Then he is hit with the reply:

Neither did the other donkey.

Finally, a chant that can only be considered very early women's liberation:
The excuse, "Boys will be boys," is met with:

And girls will be mothers.

It is hard to exaggerate the value of such advice.

Verbal Dueling

Such taunts and games seem to be universal. A special form, called "verbal dueling" has become a specialty within anthropology and linguistics. A common situation is one in which two persons face each other in the company of friends or supporters. Often some wrong has been committed and the parties thirst for a settlement, but among adolescents, it may be engaged in simply for fun or to demonstrate prowess. One person will hurl forth an insulting statement. It may then be evaluated by the supporters who look on, and the other be challenged to come back with a reply which puts the first one in his place. The challenges and responses go back and forth until one person breaks down or cannot continue. Sometimes a local magistrate may be called in to judge who has won, or to bring an end to what could otherwise develop into a serious quarrel, with resultant bloodshed.

What is interesting to us is that these contests are often embarrassment duels, attempts, as it were, to "out-embarrass" the other, to say something so cutting that the other cannot think of a good or appropriately embarrassing thing to say in return. They become tests of poise, and reputations may be won or lost on the outcome. Sometimes they take on a life of their own and people forget about the quarrel that originally brought the two parties together. The people watch the duel, as if it were a staged performance to be evaluated on artistic grounds.

Studies by sociologist William Labov in the inner city in the U. S. have unearthed a rich mine of material, suggesting the importance of ingenuity and imagination. Such verbal exchanges are sometimes called "playing the dozens." In East Coast cities, they are known as "sounding" or "signifying" whereas on the West Coast, preferred terms are "cutting" or "chopping."

Here are some examples of challenges and responses:

    I. Bel's mother bought her clothes from Ohrbach's.
All front and no back!
    II. You get your shoes from Buster Brown—brown on the top and all busted on the bottom!

After expressions of admiration from teammates, an exchange might continue:

    I. Eh, eh, your mother so skinny she could split through a needle's eye!
    II. Your mother's so skinny, about that skinny, she can get in a Cheerioat and say, "Hula hoop! Hula hoop!"

Other exchanges may be more explicit:

I. Fuck you.
II. Yeh, that would be the best one you ever had.

Embarrassment contests of this kind test and train persons in their ability to keep their cool and to control their emotions. They must use their wits to maintain poise and exhibit self-control.

It is difficult not to see such games as having major significance in preparing persons for adult social life, especially for the stressful times when a loss of self-control can lead to defeat and deprivation. Humans, of all creatures, are most dependent on their brains, rather than their brute strength and raw emotions. Through repeated embarrassment in growing up (when it is safe since it is "just a game"), persons are more likely to develop skill in the use of their intelligence to solve their problems. In a world in which we seem to be getting ready to destroy our enemies and ourselves by force, that can hardly be considered a minor contribution.

THE CASE FOR EMBARRASSMENT

Embarrassment can cause a lot of trouble, and it hurts. Now we begin to see that it can also be very useful, and a great help to survival in the modern world. We must, then, distinguish two kinds of embarrassing situations:

1. Situations where embarrassment *gets in the way*, and interrupts important events. For those situations, we need tools

to help us overcome the embarrassment, reduce the pain, and restore things to right again.

2. Situations where embarrassment is *desirable* as when it helps unmask fraud, or helps in the process of growing up. For those situations we will want to make sure embarrassment works effectively but doesn't have painful side effects we can prevent.

Most of my attention is going to be on the first situation, for it is where we need help most: doing something to manage embarrassment and reduce the pain. That is the concern in the next chapter where we ask: what causes embarrassment? But as we go along trying to control embarrassment, we must recognize embarrassment for the very human thing it is. When the late President John F. Kennedy was still a young senator, he was famous for his wit and his ability to give inspired speeches. He seemed never at a loss for an appropriate reply, and given his patrician origins, it was hard to imagine that such a man might ever be embarrassed. On one occasion, an admiring reporter asked him what he thought of just before he stood up to speak. What did he do to get himself in the proper mood – did he think of a line from Shakespeare, or perhaps of speeches of the famous orators of history?

"No," answered Kennedy, "I just check to be sure my fly is zipped up." Suddenly the distinguished senator had become more human, facing the same problems of getting ready that any person does before any occasion. He too could become embarrassed, and had the wisdom to recognize it.

Chapter 4

The Causes of Embarrassment

Four conditions are necessary for you to feel embarrassed.

1. A failure or problem occurs for which you are responsible which you should have been able to handle or prevent.

2. Others become aware of that failure or problem. Usually they see it before their very eyes, or you think they do.

3. You value their opinion or feeling about you.

4. The failure or problem happens too quickly for prevention or repair.

There are complications that can set in as well. For example, those persons whose opinion you value may also get embarrassed as they witness your embarrassment. Perhaps they were responsible for training you as when a piano teacher gets embarrassed at her pupil's error at a public piano recital. Or they may be close to you socially and identify with you as when a person feels embarrassed for his or her spouse's display of drunkenness at a party. Embarrassment can act like a contagious disease affecting all in a social gathering who will turn their faces away and wish the awful thing had never happened. We'll take up these fascinating possibilities later on. For now, look at the basic conditions.

YOU'RE RESPONSIBLE.

There's nothing simple about responsibility. Lawyers and courts have a lot of trouble with liability and volumes of learned doctrine have been written about it. In everyday life we all have a common-sense notion about it. When people back their car against the side of your car in a supermarket parking lot, you decide immediately that they are responsible even though they protest that they were distracted by their crying 3-year old child. You feel they should have paid attention anyhow. On the other hand, you do not hold small children responsible for wandering out onto the street nor sick people for failing to show up for work.

What about inherited or just plain physical blemishes such as big ears, baldness, or being too short or too tall? Consider the reply of a 15 year old Swedish girl to researchers' Ronald and Juliette Goldman's question on what embarrassed her about her body:

> (You) feel safer with clothes on. (Persons) may have too big breasts and be an early maturer, and you don't want to be teased.

Why should she fear teasing when she is hardly "responsible" in the ordinary sense for her breasts? But embarrassment is anything which interferes with the ongoing interaction, and if you bring it into the situation you will be held responsible for whatever happens. If her breasts distract others she will feel embarrassed and the others may too. It is cruel but until we change persons' attitudes, the body we are stuck with will remain a source of many embarrassments.

OTHERS ARE AWARE OF IT.

You rarely get embarrassed when you are alone, though sometimes it can suddenly strike you in thinking back on something you once did. Many older persons relate to me they still feel awful about something embarrassing they did years ago when they were teenagers. You can be alone when you look down and discover you have been walking around in public with your zipper open wide or you see in the mirror that food is caught in your front teeth. Such embarrassment are rare. Usually there is an audience and that is the trouble.

Sociologist Andre Modigliani had his experimental subjects do anagrams for use in a crossword puzzle. Some anagrams were impossible to do, others were very easy. The object of the test was to see if persons who were told they had done poorly in teams would feel embarrassed since they would cause their whole team to fail. Some were allowed to discover they had failed in private. Others were told by a person posing as a task supervisor that they had failed.

Reported embarrassment was much less when the subjects were alone than when a supervisor *told* them they had failed. Subjects who were told also engaged in much less eye contact and made a lot more attempts at "facework," that is, trying to improve

61

prove their image. For instance some blamed poor performance on the lighting, others knocked the task itself ("For my money solving anagrams is pretty meaningless and boring."). Others simply denied failure ("I doubt anyone could solve those in 10 minutes."). This last answer was often true but that didn't stop them from feeling embarrassed.

Another study by psychologists Jeffrey M. Jackson and Bibb Latané found that what they call "stage fright" got progressively worse as the size of the audience increased. On the other hand it decreased if you performed with other persons rather than all alone. They speculate that when you have to perform with a group (they report on a campus talent show), the responsibility is diffused since it is harder to pin the blame for the sour note on you. When you are alone, all doubt is removed.

What is it about an audience that makes things so terrible? That brings us the third embarrassment condition.

EMBARRASSMENT CONDITION 3

YOU VALUE THE AUDIENCE'S FEELINGS.

When you do something stupid you might not even be aware of it. If someone sees you do it and you are concerned that *he* thinks it's stupid, you then get embarrassed.

Take something we all do, forgetting someone's name. That's embarrassing because our names are precious to us and we know they are. When we hurry to assure the other person that "no offense" was intended or try to cover with a joke we are expressing our concern for the other person's opinion about us.

In one study, the experimenters asked subjects how they would feel having to sing the national anthem in front of an audience of professors and graduate students from the university music department as opposed to an audience of partially tone deaf students. Subjects said they'd feel far more tense and nervous in front of the high status audience, a finding that several others have reported in their studies. The more an audience is likely to be able to pass judgment on you, the more embarrassed are you likely to feel.

Suppose the audience is anonymous and you never expect to see them again. Would you have any reason to feel embarrassed then?

You can answer that question yourself by remembering how you act when you and a friend get on an elevator. You usually show concern for the feelings of others by modulating your voice or even remaining quiet. Should you feel an urge to burp (or worse) you usually suppress it though you will never see these people again. Studies show we are concerned even about total strangers we brush against accidentally. One of my cases reports that he apologized to a tree trunk he had backed into while waiting for a bus.

Why should we be concerned about strangers? It turns out that we are concerned at every moment that all people, even strangers, see us as persons who can be counted on to behave in a decent respectable manner. Those who do not or deliberately offend are felt to be "uncouth", at war with society, and at the least "should see a shrink."

Am I overdoing it? Take this test. Next time you and a friend board an elevator continue your conversation in just as loud a voice as before. If the stares do not bother you, then go one step further. Instead of patiently watching the floor numbers go by, turn around and face the back of the elevator. (Don't expect me to put up bail for you.) We do value others' opinions which is why embarrassment is almost always public.

But then it follows that we should not get embarrassed in private situations where we are with those we trust not to evaluate us. That is just what happens according to Professor of Communication Michael Schudson. He calls attention to the fact that embarrassment rarely occurs when people are relaxing at home with loved ones or enjoying a coffee break with professional colleagues. Another situation of little or no embarrassment occurs when people are so caught up in what they are doing that they are unaware of others, as with a couple so much in love that they can't keep from looking into one another's eyes.

Something like that is operating with persons who lose themselves in religious ecstasy or in the passion of devotion to a charismatic leader. The only person's evaluation they care about is the leader's. They will carry on in any public place without a trace of embarrassment.

In reporting on my work on embarrassment, I am occasionally asked if there are any people who are simply unembarrassable whatever the situation. All of us have occasionally met someone so blasé, so full of savoir faire, so much in command of himself that we imagine he would never be embarrassed. My own research leads me to doubt that. Someone who seems in command in public may be much less adroit among his own friends. He is careful to prepare himself for public appearances as if he were getting ready for a performance.

My work did turn up one kind of person who seems embarrass-proof: one of unimpeachable status such as a high born aristocrat. Such persons suffer little embarrassment since their position is so lofty that other person's evaluations are simply of no account.

Such was the case for British King Edward Vll who on being chided (mildly we presume) by his valet for dressing in clothes a "bit old fashioned," growled to his unfortunate valet:

I *am* the fashion.

Such persons are very rare, especially in the modern world but they have existed. In rigid class or caste societies, aristocrats felt little or no discomfort in carrying on intimate activities, even sex, in the presence of servants and other low status retainers.

Nowadays high status persons who are far from being embarrass-proof have an additional protection. When they might get embarrassed, lower status persons are very careful to protect them by pretending it did not happen. In large businesses or governmental bureaucracies, lower staff may fear punishment if they show too much awareness of some flub the boss has made. The rest of us have to deal with embarrassment on our own.

EMBARRASSMENT CONDITION 4

IT HAPPENS FAST

Usually embarrassment exposes for all the world to see something about you which you would rather they would not see. This means that if we can prevent it we do. However if it happens suddenly before we get a chance to prevent it we are then stuck.

A man crosses his legs and discovers that he has put on mismatched socks with the result that he worries that others will make fun of him. Or you are in the woods cutting down a Christmas tree on land you thought had been condemned for a superhighway. A forest official stops to inform you that is not the case.

65

In both cases what we have is a sudden discovery of something about you or the world that you did not know but which you and others feel you should have known. This suddenness is very common in embarrassment since otherwise you might have been able to avoid the problem. If you had dressed more slowly you would have noticed the mismatch. If the road was many miles long you might have wondered why there were no others cutting down trees. It is this suddenness that gives to much embarrassment the character of exposure, of the feeling that you have instantly been stripped and that everyone is looking at you.

WHAT HAPPENS NEXT

There you are. You have exposed something about yourself in front of persons who may be questioning their previously favorable opinion about you. Up to that point you have been moving along smoothly, your usual confident self.

Now instead of moving along you must stop. The very fact that others are appraising you forces you to start paying attention to your behavior. You begin to seek desperately to explain or for a way out of the situation. It is as if you were suddenly shoved onto a stage without rehearsal and forced to perform in front of a critical audience. Since you don't know what to do, your behavior becomes erratic, gawky and inhibited. You look for help to that critical audience or wish they would go away.

Your body is no help either. It actually makes things worse. You perspire, drool, stutter, your muscles grow weak, and you blush. Is there anybody more miserable than you?

EVERYONE'S LOOKING

The key to embarrassment is the self-consciousness that it creates. You sense yourself not as a subject who does things under your control, but as an object being manipulated. It is hardly surprising that one of the commonest settings for embarrassment is the medical examination when we must willingly cooperate in allowing ourselves to be stared at, questioned, doubted, appraised, flipped over, probed, touched, and poked at, all under bright lights when we have few resources to defend ourselves.

In other situations anything that calls attention to us may similarly become a source of embarrassment. It may be a prominent body feature (nose, ears, hair, largeness, smallness, tallness, shortness, feet, arms), anything different about our clothes, any unusual feature of our car, or apartment, or anything identified with us such as a child, a dog or someone we happen to be with at the moment. As long as that someone or something is seen (or could be seen) by others as not quite right, as long as those others are important to us then we stop paying attention to what we were doing and start paying attention to ourselves and what others may be thinking of us. While we do that our behavior comes to a stop. Now the problem is embarrassment itself—the blushing, the stumbling, the interruption, the sheer fact that while we are embarrassed, we are no longer able to carry on.

CAN EMBARRASSMENT BE IGNORED?

It is one thing to be embarrassed over something serious, as when an industrial product we manufacture turns out to threaten people's health, or when a government official embarrasses his colleagues by a personal scandal. But so many embarrassments are over what seem like such trivial matters. I can imagine people saying: So suppose my socks do not match, who cares? So what if my hair is not combed and brushed in what passes for the current fashion? That does not affect my true worth as a dress designer (or lover), does it? What if my car is an old, beat-up heap? If people don't like it, they don't have to ride in it. What if I have forgotten to bring my speech? People probably would have been bored by it anyhow.

These claims have validity but they all have a certain note of defensiveness about them. They all run up against the third condition in our model—concern for the feelings and opinions of other persons. If you *really* do not care what others may think, then you *are* armor-proof against embarrassment. That is rare. Whether we like it or not, the feelings of others are a part of the world in which we live.

This is not simply a matter of politeness. Others affect us in two key ways that none of us escapes:

1. *Other persons are the source of our reputations.* Because of the way they see us, they think of us as certain kinds of people. This leads them to treat us in certain ways either kindly, with concern and respect or as objects of indifference or contempt. We cannot function at all unless we have a basic feeling of self-respect, a sense that others see us as persons fully entitled to be treated honorably.

2. *To attain our goals, we need the assistance and cooperation of other persons.* In all but the simplest acts persons work together and divide up the joint product. This means that for you to get to your own ends, however private, you are going to have to call on others. They in turn will only respond willingly if they value you or think highly of you.

Mismatched socks may be trivial but not if customers or supervisors interpret such carelessness as lack of concern for detail or sloppiness in preparation. Hair and how it is taken care of is also interpreted and although it does not correlate precisely with "true worth," persons act as if it does, or at least those who might hire you for a job or want to work with you often do. Cars are considered to reflect a person's judgment and taste. Failing to deliver an expected speech can cause chaos on the part of those who planned the occasion when the speech was to be delivered. You have spoiled that occasion, with loss of reputation or sales, or a sense of having been let down by persons who were looking to you for leadership. The occasion itself may be trivial, but it is what the embarrassment may say about the kind of person you are and how you treat others that is important.

Can embarrassment be ignored? For most of us most of the time, the answer is it *can*, but the costs will be high.

WHEN DO WE GET EMBARRASSED?

We are now ready to see what it is that gives rise to embarrassment. Embarrassment occurs when there is some question about someone's identity, image, or reputation. Either that identity or image is *inappropriate* or else it becomes *discredited*.

INAPPROPRIATE IDENTITIES

An inappropriate identity is one that disqualifies you for participation or even for being there at all. A very common one occurs when a man wanders into an area reserved for women (or vice versa). Sexual identity is the most pervasive of all identities and can rarely be ignored. On a recent plane trip I found myself

69

seated next to an elderly woman who had never flown before. After lunch she arose to go to the toilet, of which there happened to be only one in that part of the plane. I heard her ask the flight attendant where the "ladies toilet" was. She merely pointed to the toilet.

"But," the woman said in alarm, "I just saw a man come out of there!"

The flight attendant patiently, and with a slight smile, explained that the toilet was used by everyone. Instead of being mollified the woman became increasingly upset. She returned to her seat muttering to those who could hear: "I can't go into a man's bathroom. I just can't." The poor woman sat in her seat, undoubtedly suffering, until the plane landed when she rushed out the door to a toilet labeled WOMEN where she felt she could present an appropriate identity.

Sometimes persons become embarrassed when an inappropriate identity is thrust upon them. They then cannot play their accustomed roles. In traditional gender relations, for example, the big handsome he-man is supposed to the be the one who provides help to the supposedly weak little-woman. An Israeli study confirmed this stereotype. Social psychologists Arie Nadler, Rina Shapira and Shulamit Ben-Itzhak reported that 91.7% of female subjects asked for help in solving a mystery puzzle when the helper was a physically attractive male. But when male subjects faced an attractive female helper, only 6% would ask her for help. The experimenters did not ask whether subjects felt more embarrassed but they did report they felt unpleasant or tense.

A published anecdotal report makes the result clearer. A woman tells what happened when she got onto an elevator ahead of a football player who lived in her building. Seeing he was loaded with groceries, she hurriedly held back the door for him. She writes:

He was so embarrassed he couldn't even say thank-you.

There are literally hundreds of situations in which an inappropriate identity gives rise to embarrassment. Some are forgetting your money when it comes time to pay the bill (money is part of your identity as a customer), wearing a dress identical to that of another woman at a cocktail party, for men wearing something very different from that of all the other men (when you didn't mean to be different), and the most common of all mispronouncing or forgetting someone's name when you are the host who is introducing people.

Discrediting A Claimed Identity

Here you do present an appropriate identity, but it is discredited. A speaker may be doing fine but then is thrown by a question or a heckler whom he cannot handle. A wealthy relative's gift of a self-portrait may have to be dragged out for display before the relative arrives. Otherwise the identity the couple is trying to maintain, falsely, as loving relatives, will be discredited. Perhaps the commonest discreditation occurs when your chair slips, or you knock over the wine on a linen tablecloth raising questions about your gracefulness or control of movements. There are more situations: the microphone fails, your car stalls in traffic, you drop the bowling ball, or allow a match to burn down until it burns your fingers.

Clothing seems to present unending opportunities for embarrassment. Stained neckties, tears, underwear peeking out, and all the horrible things that can happen to zippers. Then there is the body, which must always be in a state of readiness to act, and its appearance must make this clear. Any evidence of unreadiness or clumsiness may be embarrassing. Some examples include stumbling, trembling, or drooling as well as the tragic failures of body control that accompany some diseases and old age. Some of my material on the elderly suggests that they are more embarrassed than many believe. Failures of hearing, the inability to hold a tea cup steady or having to use a walker may be felt to be so embarrassing that many prefer to be alone so that no one can witness those disabilities. Some of the loneliness we associate with problems older persons face may be self-imposed.

THE "BAR" IN EMBARRASSMENT

There's a reason why the syllable "bar" is there. "Bar" has the meaning it has in "barrier" or when you find yourself barred from entering a closed place. It means "stop."

That's just what embarrassment does and why attention must be paid to it. It stops the action while we stop to repair the damage. As we have seen, one of the reasons identity problems are so important is that they often hold up some vital activity. A tongue-tied public speaker is not only personally embarrassed. He also wastes the time of those who have come to hear him. Your car stalling in traffic not only reflects on you as a negligent person (perhaps you are out of gas or should have had the car checked) but in addition it stops traffic which may be dangerous.

A man reported to me of driving on an expressway with a friend while holding a lighted cigarette in one hand. He accidentally dropped the cigarette between his legs leading to frantic efforts to recover it.

Funny? Yes as a story told by a comedian. But in his case he almost lost control of the car forcing him to pull over to the shoulder he could not only recover the cigarette but his composure as well. Something trivial had turned into a possible matter of life and death. Other less serious matters are just as embarrassing. We can get carried away by something and overdo it. Students on a bus taking them and their teachers to a basketball game can become so boisterous that they forget teachers are present and begin expressing their true feelings about them. As they suddenly realize the teachers can hear, the blushing of the students brings everything to a halt as they wonder if they have lost their future chances to be taken to games.

You may start to tell a bedtime story to a child and get carried away in describing the horrible dragon as you leap up and down for dramatic effect. The child may love it but then you discover you are being observed by another adult who looks on amused at your acting talents. Even though he will probably urge you to go right on, the mood has been spoiled and you are likely to hurry on to the story's conclusion.

Embarrassment is like a cold hard stage light that exposes us to the judgment of others. The judgment may be unfair but the sheer fact of judgment itself puts us on the spot as we hurry to make excuses or justify what we are doing even if nothing is really needed. Each of us cares too much about our identities to simply ignore what has happened.

Chapter 5

Shyness and Shame

Shy, ashamed and embarrassed persons often act similarly. They lower their eyes, their hearts pound and they "wish they could die." But in spite of similarities, the causes are very different.

SHYNESS

Shy persons are afraid of and try to avoid situations where they run the risk of being thought inadequate by others no matter what they do. That makes shyness a psychological fact, maybe a part of personality or even a disability if severe enough.

If you are afraid of and avoid people, you will avoid unpleasant encounters and enjoy your own company undisturbed. But you will also miss out on the great "strokes" people give each other, you will not meet interesting people and you may have career problems. Even those who work alone such as writers and painters have to deal with editors and dealers.

If you are shy and it really bothers you, then you may profit from psychological or counseling help. Much can be done.

Embarrassment is something else. Psychologists Mark R. Leary and Barry R. Schlenker point out that shyness is different from embarrassment in that shyness occurs even when nothing has happened that reflects unfavorably on you. But you fear something might.

But with embarrassment something has happened that casts doubt on the image you are presenting. That can happen to shy and non-shy people alike. Take slips of the tongue, for instance. Shy person s may find the possibility of that happening so painful that they avoid even talking. Non-shy persons simply get embarrassed and go on as best they can.

Here are two examples of leading political figures who suffered embarrassment, one is a former United States Secretary of State, the second the President.

The Secretary of State, Alexander Haig was telling reporters of meetings between the late Egyptian President Anwar Sadat and President Reagan. Haig said:

> "During discussions involving Egypt's future, President Sadat described very poignantly to President Nixon the diffi-culty he had....the difficulty he had.... " Haig said, pausing at the rising laughter. He was told he had substituted Nixon for Reagan in the Oval Office discussions with Sadat. "Did I?" Haig said, "Oh, my heavens."

I doubt than anyone would have thought of Secretary Haig as a shy person, but he was certainly embarrassed. Like embar-rassed persons generally, he stumbled on trying to recover:

> "That's because I'm thinking ahead (to what ? Nixon's return?), you see, and not keeping my feet on the ground, thinking what I'm going to say next."

A 1993 newspaper report after a summit meeting between President Clinton and Russian President Boris Yeltsin was head-lined:

CLINTON EMBARRASSED BY FORGOTTEN NOTES

In the privacy of their summit talks, President Clinton shared a diplomatic secret with Russian President Boris Yeltsin: "When the Japanese, say yes to us, they often mean no."

The White House was embarrassed when Russian-language notes of the conversation, left behind on the table after a Clinton-Yeltsin dinner Saturday in Vancouver, B. C., were found by a local T.V. reporter.

The newspaper goes on to relate hurried attempts at "damage control" by top government officials.

Here again, I have not heard that either President Clinton or Boris Yeltsin are shy persons, but the incident still was embarrassing. Embarrassment can happen to the strong-minded as well as the shy.

Nor is it true to say that shy persons are simply those who are always embarrassed. Psychologist Philip G. Zimbardo, an expert on shyness as well as the leading researcher, found in a national survey of nearly 5000 persons that shyness is quite common. Some 40% of his respondents consider themselves shy. It does vary, being very high among the Japanese and very low among Israelis. He quotes research suggesting that shyness is probably commoner in cultures, such as ours which emphasize individualism and prize success.

However common, shy persons are those who, because of their personalities, find it uncomfortable to be in the presence of others. Zimbardo states that they find small talk difficult and fear people. One result is that they avoid people and along with that, will avoid all the embarrassment that everyone else is exposed to. Zimbardo provides a quotation from Cornell MacNeil, baritone star of the San Francisco opera. MacNeil tells of being shy at parties. At a dinner party held following the opening of an opera, Rock Cornish hens were served:

> They were slippery from having been held over too long. I was afraid if I ate mine that it would slip off the plate and down the décolleté dress of one of the ladies opposite. So I only ate the rice.

We can see that since shy persons may, like Mr. MacNeil, seek to avoid potentially embarrassing situations, they may end up experiencing no more or even less embarrassment than do other persons. Their problem is to deal with their shyness.

That is why we must leave shyness to psychologists and other counselors. Embarrassment in contrast, is no illness or deficiency. Everyone faces it, some more than others. Above all it is not something requiring treatment like shyness, if the shyness is disabling. People, shy or not, can learn to handle their embarrassments as we shall see.

IS SHAME DIFFERENT FROM EMBARRASSMENT?

Social psychologists Mary K. Babcock and John Sabini designed experiments to find out. They first asked students at the University of Pennsylvania to describe instances when they'd felt embarrassed and when they'd felt ashamed. Based on these descriptions, Babcock and Sabini drew up scenarios and then asked samples of students whether they could tell them apart. They used many examples and came up with strong findings. Here are two of their scenarios.

You've been flirting on the phone with someone you are really interested in. You've been talking for almost two hours. As soon as you hang up, the phone rings again. You are sure that it must be your "sweetheart" again. You say in a sexy voice, "I knew that you wouldn't be able to stand being without me for long." You expect to hear a sexy reply back. You get a reply and you recognize the voice, but it's your mother's.

Your best friend, Jane, confides to you that her brother has just been committed to a mental institution. She is very upset about it. She tells you that you are the only person she has told and she asks you not to tell anyone. You give her your word that you will not. You are shocked and don't know what to think, so you tell your friend and make him promise not to tell. He tells his friend and the word gets around. One night you are all sitting in the lounge and someone comes up to Jane and says, "I'm really sorry to hear about your brother. You must feel awful." Jane breaks down in tears. She looks at you on the way out.

The students had little difficulty in saying they would feel embarrassed about sexy talk with their mother and ashamed about the violation of confidence, though there was some overlap.

What is the difference? The experimenters conducted other tests to check out whether it was a difference in seriousness, in whether it was intentional or not and other possible differences. They conclude that the key difference is that the sexy words to the mother showed the person as acting out of character, as just not the sort of thing they say to their mother, though just right for a lover.

On the other hand, violation of a confidence is, in Babcock and Sabini's words "a deviation from what (one) takes to be an

79

objective and universal ideal of what it is to be a worthy person." Being sexy is not being unworthy. It's just what lovers should be to one another. It just happens to be wrong for your mother.

Shame arises when your realize that you have not lived up to an ideal. You have done something dishonorable which is really beneath you. If you fail to win in a competition which you might have won if you had trained harder, if you fail to honor an obligation to others who were depending on you, if you cheat those you love, you may well feel ashamed and unworthy.

Shame does not depend on whether anyone finds out about it. Even if Jane had not looked at you as she left, you might still feel ashamed because you know you let her down. Some persons feel so ashamed that they commit suicide never telling anyone. We learn of their shame by reading the suicide note.

Drs. Babcock and Sabini looked into the matter of secrecy also. They asked their respondents whether they would tell others about the embarrassment or the shame. They found persons much more likely to tell others of the embarrassment and much less likely to tell of their shame.

That is not so surprising. I found that many of those telling or writing me of their embarrassing experience love to tell me with all the gory details. I often have to stop people since they start to go into intimate details I'd rather not hear about.

But shameful experiences? It's hard to imagine anyone, even a friend, coming up to us and saying: "Let me tell you about this shameful thing I did..."

In a nutshell, shame occurs when you feel unworthy. No one need ever know but you. On the other hand, you get embarrassed when your presentation of your self, your identity or image to others is out of character. You present an inappropriate identity or one discredited by what happens, as when a robber wrote out his demand for money on the back of a bank deposit slip which he pushed across the counter to the teller. Unfortunately the deposit slip was from his own account with his name, address and telephone number conveniently printed on the other side for the benefit of the police.

APPROPRIATE EMBARRASSMENT

Shyness is rarely something persons feel is an appropriate way to act. Most shy persons cannot really control it one way or another. Shameful acts are never really appropriate though there are situations where others feel you should be ashamed of yourself. Even there, if you could, you would probably not want others to know about it.

Embarrassment is different from both shyness and shame in that there are occasions when it not only happens but when it should happen and when it is okay or even desirable for others to know about it .

In a newspaper column I have before me, a famous doctor responds to the anguished appeal of a mother who asks what she can do about the fact that her "15 year old daughter is terribly embarrassed by excess hair around the mouth and face." He calls the problem "hirsutism," attributes it to a hormonal imbalance and suggests seeing an endocrinologist or trying electrolysis.

I have no quarrel with the doctor who obviously knows more than I do about such matters. If the hair excess is really severe, then medical treatment may be just what is needed. But what the doctor should remember is that teen-agers are notoriously prone to embarrassment about everything that proclaims their emerging maturity. There is hair in lots of places, growth of breasts, changes in shape, menstruation and any signs that might show it, clothes that do not fit or are too revealing and a hundred other changes.

Teen-agers can be helped through this difficult period but above all comes this reminder: EMBARRASSMENT AT THAT AGE IS NORMAL. It does not mean anything is wrong with you, or in many cases, that any doctor's help is required. A modest amount of hair on the face is far from unattractive and in many cultures may even be regarded as beautiful. Whatever the case, changes at such a time are normal and should happen. There are ways to reduce the discomfort persons feel, as we show in the next chapter. Be assured the embarrassment itself is normal.

The teen-ager's problem points to a more general condition. Whenever a person does something new or enters a new situation, embarrassment is hardly surprising, even desirable. When a person asks for someone's hand in marriage, asks for a loan or seeks a promotion or new job, it is appropriate to exhibit some flustering or uncertainty as to how to behave.

Asking a woman to marry him, how should a man behave? Perhaps such famous cases as Mickey Rooney or the late George Jessel, who had a lot of experience, proposing may have become routine. Having done it so frequently, they may have worked out a smooth way of handling it.

But for most men it should be a grand and rather disturbing occasion. They should be excited, unsure of themselves, stumble or stutter, not really knowing what to say. A proposal does not really admit of much rehearsal or of being carried off with consummate grace. If a man talks as if he were simply reciting memorized lines from a script, the woman is bound to feel insulted as though he treats the matter with no more concern than he might to ordering his dinner.

CAUGHT DOING SOMETHING WRONG

Another occasion in which embarrassment is appropriate occurs when you have been "caught sinning" or doing something you should not have done. Obvious examples come to mind of congressmen and senators who are found to have been willing to use their influence to help with legislation on behalf of foreign clients. A more amusing example occurred recently when it was revealed that a University of Missouri basketball center, who had told police he had been shot in the arm by a masked gunman, had instead accidentally shot himself in the arm. His story was fabricated to conceal his embarrassment, but most felt that an athlete *should* have been embarrassed to have done such a klutzy thing.

The pilot who was responsible for the following experience should have felt embarrassed. The news story reported:

TAMPA, Fla. (AP)—The Boeing 727 broke through the low-hanging overcast, bumped to an easy landing and rolled to a stop. "Welcome to Tampa International Airport," a smiling attendant told the 90 passengers.

But Delta Air Lines' Flight 604 was at MacDill Air Force Base, eight miles to the south. "We have inadvertently landed at MacDill," the pilot announced after a few minutes on the ground.

. . . one passenger, Lakeland, Fla. businessman Joe Gandolfo, said he knew what was happening even if the pilot didn't.

"I yelled out, 'The guy's going to the wrong airport,' and everybody thought I was nuts," Gandolfo said. "The stewardess told me to sit down and shut up.

"It was the dumbest thing I've ever seen. We could have been killed," Gandolfo said.

We are not told what the airline had to say to the pilot but probably embarrassment was the least of his worries.

We all get caught from time to time. A common experience is discussing someone critically only to realize that person is right behind you and probably overheard what you said. Or persons can try to sneak through the express line at the supermarket with more than the allowable number of items, only to be stared at by others waiting in line. In such situations, it is appropriate for a person to feel embarrassed, to blush and show all the unhappy symptoms that go with it. It is all a kind of penalty for not being alive to the situation or not acting as you should.

But even when you deserve it, do you have to just sit and suffer? An experiment shows that you can do something, you can make amends.

MAKING AMENDS

A social psychologist, Robert Apsler, asked a sample of student subjects to perform various embarrassing tasks in front of another student they were told was observing them from behind one-way glass. They were asked to:

1. turn on a tape recorder and dance to the music
2. laugh for 30 seconds as if they had just heard a joke
3. sing the Star Spangled Banner
4. imitate a 5 year old having a temper tantrum because he does not want to go to kindergarten.

They were told this was an experiment in "impression formation," and that the observer behind the one-way glass would be forming an impression of how the subject performed.

A second group of student subjects was asked to do things that were probably not embarrassing (turn on the tape recorder and simply listen to the recording, walk around the room, read a book to themselves and count up to 50.) It was assumed these students would feel little embarrassment. But since just being observed is often felt to be embarrassing, Dr. Apsler made sure by bringing in a *third* group who were not asked to do anything at all. They would form a Control Group.

The person they thought was observing them from behind the one-way glass was a "stooge," a student hired by the social psychologist to help out with the experiment. After each subject had done as he or she was requested, the stooge-observer came into the room and acted like a student who was waiting for the psychologist to come back and tell them what to do next. After a minute or two, the stooge pulled out a sheet of paper with the days of the month printed on it and asked if the subject would be willing to offer help in a class assignment he or she had for another class. The help involved a boring task, requiring that the subject spend from one half to one hour every day for up to 20 *days* or more, filling out a long questionnaire.

The experiment was designed to see if embarrassment made any difference in people's willingness to help others. Here are the findings:

Average Time Persons
Would Give To Help Out
in a Boring Task

Group 1 (High Embarrassment) ....14.9 days
Group 2 (Little Embarrassment) ....8.7 days
Group 3 (Control Group: No Embarrassment)............5.0 days

In other words, the more embarrassed persons feel, the more willing are they to help out. Other experiments support this finding. Embarrassment may lead to a blow to a person's self-esteem. The person is then willing to do something, even if it is unpleasant, to restore that self-esteem. It is as if one were saying to the other: "I'm not so inept or so foolish as I just looked to you. I'm really quite a decent and capable person. To prove it, I'll help you out in whatever you ask me to do."

To be embarrassed is to say that you are normal, that you are a decent deserving person, aware of your responsibilities and totally dependable. A study by social psychologist Jerome Sattler compared students and adults with hospitalized schizophrenics. The schizophrenics showed little sign of being able to be embarrassed at all, even when they understood the instructions. The key element is awareness of others and concern for their feelings about you, capacities which schizophrenics lack or do not value. To be embarrassed is also to announce that you are normal, and that is hardly a bad thing.

When to be Glad You Are Embarrassed

Most of the time we are pained by our embarrassments and want to just get through them. Even to be assured it is normal or to try to preserve our reputation by making amends doesn't make it any the less painful.

There are times when we should actually be grateful to be embarrassed. Social psychologist Mary K. Babcock provides the clue when she calls embarrassment "a window on the self." What she means is that embarrassment reveals something about us not only to others but also to ourselves. That self-discovery can lead to self-change and improvement.

A woman who suddenly discovers she has forgotten to bring an essential document to a meeting may feel devastated as her colleagues glare at her for wasting their time. An athlete may be forced to admit to himself that he can no longer do 20 miles on the jogging track but instead suffers embarrassment as younger persons shout greetings as they pass him by.

But these can be occasions for positive self-discovery when they lead those persons to change their behavior, re-assess their skills or turn to activities they can handle. The woman who forgot the document can make it a regular practice to make a list of needed papers and notes in advance of important meetings, and the athlete can consider turning to managing or other professions.

A special kind of embarrassment is faced by persons in big business or government who find the job and technology changing in ways they cannot deal with. Often it is not a personal failing but job erosion from company mergers or market forces that drive employers to make unpleasant choices. Then persons may not be actually discharged but face demotion in subtle ways.

Sociologist Douglas M. More writes of general forepersons who are reduced to departmental forepersons, but at no reduction in salary. One development engineer was given an assignment to a routine job in plant engineering. Some executives were simply bypassed in seniority and others discovered there were more steps above them in the company hierarchy. All these changes make the persons feel uncomfortable and often embarrassed as they tried to "explain" to others that all was well.

Sociologist Rosabeth Moss Kanter in her studies of a large corporation found that persons experiencing such changes of status, even where subtle, might depress their aspirations in the company, withdraw their commitment or even bad mouth the company. Yet many found that the signals they received were messages providing "a window on the self" leading them to take a new view of themselves and what was possible. Some became trainers of young persons and gave them the benefit of mentoring and advice on life in the corporation and how to make it. It was not common but a way of discovering something they could do and do well.

In another study sociologist Burton Clark found that junior or community colleges provided similar chances for young people who had "messed up" in high school to get a second chance. Although often they enrolled with unrealistic hopes that they could soon make up for losses in high school, many soon found the going too rough. But with the help of counselors, they might find new careers they had never considered. Persons who had once thought they would be lawyers found they might have satisfying careers as legal paraprofessionals. Some who once thought of being dentists but lacked the science courses discovered they might still become dental assistants. In a real sense, the community college enabled persons to get over what they had once thought of as their embarrassing school performance and low self worth. Their embarrassment had been unpleasant but it led them to take stock of their true abilities and in the end, be able to lead satisfying lives after all.

WHAT IS NEXT?

We have been talking about embarrassment, the bad and good things it does. But even when it is a good thing, it is unpleasant. It still leads us to stumble, to blush and wish we could vanish.

What we are now going to look at is what you can do to overcome these side effects and deal with embarrassment itself. Sometimes we can prevent or hide it. If not, you can use four strategies: make light of it, change its meaning, show others that what happened is not the real you or get others to help you get through the embarrassment. You can even do all four at once in intriguing combinations. Let us see how.

PART II

Avoiding
Embarrassment

The very suddenness of embarrassment usually throws us but we can do something about it. The first step is to try to *prevent* the incident from happening.

A part of growing up consists of learning what can cause embarrassment. It ranges from untied shoelaces to unkept promises. You watch how mom or dad carefully close a fishing tackle box with a cover-latch before lifting it. You also observe what happens when they forget and all the lures and hooks go tumbling out of their neat compartments onto the wet bottom of the boat. As a teen-age girl, you discover that overhaste in putting on a swimsuit bra-top results in your providing undesired entertainment for a wildly applauding crowd of gawking boys.

Famous persons need to prepare too. As a senator, Robert Kennedy travelled to Nairobi where he was soon surrounded by a throng of admiring Kenyans. In waving he gave the crowd the familiar "thumbs up" gesture which unfortunately was the campaign symbol of the local Communist party.

When prevention fails, an alternative is to try to *hide* the incident. Sometimes you do this by simply using a newspaper to cover a yawn. Others employ more heroic measures. When orchestra conductor Jose Serebrier became "over passionate" while conducting at an Easter festival in Mexico City, his baton broke, a piece stabbing him right through his hand. Although blood spurted over the music stand and onto his white turtleneck tuxedo shirt, he managed to extract the piece of baton and finish conducting with a wad of handkerchief clutched in his hand.

From that example you can see that efforts to prevent or conceal embarrassment are not easy to come by. Still, we often can do so.

Chapter 6

Prevention

Preventing embarrassment is a lot easier than trying to recover from it. So you should try prevention if you can. When is that possible?

The most common preventable situations turn out to be the two extremes: the small ones that occur all the time and strangely, also the most important ones. For instance, we routinely seek to prevent small embarrassments when we pause to straighten our tie or look briefly in the mirror to check on makeup.

We also prevent the most important ones because those are precisely the ones that can have serious consequences that must be prevented. An epileptic for example, may be highly concerned that he will be embarrassed and embarrass others around him should he suffer a seizure in a public place. That concern may lead him to be sure to check on his medication beforehand or make sure he is in the presence of a friend or relative who knows of the problem.

I will get to some of these important ones later on. For now I want to look at the little ones which are also far more frequent.

GENERAL PREVENTIVE MOVES

In public places among those whom you care least about or whom you do not know personally the main concern is to maintain your right to go about your business unhindered. To have that right challenged can be deeply embarrassing even if the challenge is only a disapproving look.

When is your right to be present or move about in public likely to be challenged? The right is in jeopardy when your appearance or your behavior make others unsure of what you are liable to do next. That uncertainty leads to avoidance or stronger measures if you appear dangerous.

To make sure that does not happen, persons must do two things:

1. present an appropriate appearance, especially dress

and

2. make it clear that anything they do can be seen as rational.

Unintentional violations of those rules are seen as embarrassing providing a powerful pressure on us not to violate them. If successful then we prevent the embarrassment. The two rules seem obvious but how we follow them is not obvious at all. Learning how to follow those rules make up much of what we learn as children.

APPROPRIATE APPEARANCE

Appearance include much more than dress of course. Whether an unshaved man will feel embarrassed depends on the setting. Mowing his lawn on a warm Sunday is one thing. Appearing late to a business meeting called by his manager on Monday is something else. Hair braids or weaves on a young African American female may be admired and the flat-top on a

94

young male may be worn proudly. The same hairstyles on elderly African American persons may invite teasing comment.

Other aspects of body appearance such as posture, walking style, blemishes and other features vary in how embarrassing they seem. Ed Sullivan, long-time host of a variety TV show was also a newspaper columnist. On one occasion he wrote that comedian George Burns wore a toupee. When Mr. Burns complained to Mr. Sullivan for publicly revealing this embarrassing fact, Mr. Sullivan defended himself, saying:

But, George, I didn't think you'd mind.

To which Mr. Burns replied:

If I didn't mind, why would I wear a toupee?

Although appearance clearly includes more than dress, I want to focus on dress which is the most important and usually most visible part of appearance. It is easy to say that inappropriate dress is embarrassing but what is appropriate dress in public? A trip to the business area of a large city is likely to give the impression that anything goes. Closer inspection shows there is a definite order which persons recognize even while they violate it.

The order is briefly stated in the rule: *wear whatever proclaims the identity you wish to assign to yourself.* Only if identity is clear is behavior predictable. Others may not like it but they can at least anticipate what you are up to and can take account of it or ignore it as they please.

The allowable variety was nicely stated in a metaphor I heard used in a public lecture by sociologist Samuel C. Heilman who was discussing ethnic and multicultural diversity in the

United States. We never had a melting pot, he observed since that implies everyone would end up alike. A better metaphor is that of a salad. Some could be lettuce, others tomatoes, still others croutons but they combine to make up the all American salad while still retaining their own distinctive character.

For a large American city salad, we need only add to Professor Heilman's salad some strong pepper, some chunks that are hard to swallow, some ingredients you don't care for as well as others that look strange to you. Finally allow for the likelihood that some parts of the salad are not as well washed as other parts.

In the salad various persons and groups are clearly recognizable. There are upper-middle class nonworking housewives who are "dressed up" (dress or gown, full make-up, fashionable hairstyle) for a dinner or evening party. Their husbands are in suits or jackets and matching pants. Working-class persons may go out to fewer such occasions but make more informal family visits which are not defined as special occasions. Such visits may involve no change from work clothing unless such clothing is work-soiled as with painters or gardeners. They will often change to sport shirt, pants and running shoes when out to bowl as well as on family visits.

Most clothes are age-appropriate. The most striking is the near universal teen-age costume of T-shirt and jeans (shorts in warm weather) which teen-agers will wear on almost any occasion. Aging males who wish to appear "with it" may also affect jeans (usually of designer quality) though those may be complemented with a highstyle sportshirt with gold necklace and medallion or ascot scarf to conceal wrinkles or chicken neck. Any of these persons, young or old, will tolerantly note the knobby-kneed, camera-toting clusters waiting in line for their tour-guide to show them through a local sight.

The degree of toleration of variety in dress is much higher in suburban shopping areas which many persons treat as extensions of their homes. That allows a woman to shop with curlers covered by a kerchief or a man doing home repairs on a warm day to appear barechested in the local hardware store.

As any of these distinctively dressed persons hurry on their way they may choose not to notice homeless persons sitting beside bundles of bedding or beggars rattling coins inside discarded plastic cups which recently held jumbo-size Cokes. They too are part of the salad.

ORDER AMID THE DIVERSITY

It is easy to see the variety as chaotic, as implying that persons are free to wear anything they please. Sociologically that would be misleading, even wrong.

All persons must, if they are to be allowed the license to pass freely on the street or mall, follow the identity rule I stated earlier. They must wear the clothing or costume that makes it clear what identity they are claiming. So the middle-class husband *must* put on a suit and matching tie, the teen-agers don their T-shirts and the suburban housewife feels confident she can get by wearing curlers. Each is announcing: I am a middle-class male on my way to dinner, I am a teen-ager on my way to hang out at the mall or I am a suburbanite out shopping. Even the homeless person or beggar must dress like a homeless person or beggar if he or she expects an appropriate handout or toleration by the police.

All of those persons are dressed appropriately for the identity they claim. To do otherwise can be embarrassing as would be the case for a suburban housewife who turned up for anything but a brief shopping stop in evening gown and fashionable hairstyle or a beggar who tried to get handouts in a torn tuxedo jacket and ribboned pants which he got out of a dumpster. Even he might make it if he regularly wore the tuxedo making it a part of his personna and became knows as a habitue.

On the other hand, a dare-devil teen ager who turned up in tie, jacket and sharply pressed polyester pants to hang out in the mall with T-shirted friends would embarrass them even if he did not embarrass himself. He could likely only get away with it if, like the beggar in tuxedo, he could get his friends to tolerate him amusedly as their token "character," a recognizable type in some teen-age circles .

In all these cases embarrassment occurs when persons find themselves dressed differently from the tolerable standards of their group and when they care what others think about it. The fact that few dare to do so only attests to how far persons will go to prevent embarrassment.

A final point. Since con men and other frauds can count on the rest of us dressing to our various identities, we expose ourselves to be taken in by those who mimic the legitimately dressed. One dress that is familiar in busy downtown streets is that worn by the construction and street repair persons with their jackhammers and acetyline torches. We carefully walk around them or obey street detour signs so as not to disturb them at work.

It was predictable then, that a band of thieves in Melbourne, Australia would furnish themselves with this equipment as well as legally required hard hats. They proceeded to carefully gash a large hole in the wall of an antique shop where they made away with $56,000 in jewels. The news article recording the theft does not mention it but I would not be surprised if the police detoured traffic around them as they worked. By doing so the police would further compound the embarrassment they surely felt at being taken in in the first place.

RATIONAL ACTION

The Melbourne thieves have something else to teach us. They got away with it not only because they looked like construction workers but also because they were doing something that looked legitimate. Their activities appeared rational to the police and anyone else. In fact even if found out before they'd gotten away with it, what they were doing would be illegal, but still rational.

Rationality is important because only if others see what you do as rational can they anticipate what you are going to do next and take it into account. The result is that one common kind of embarrassment is to be caught doing something whose meaning is not clear.

Take talking for example. It is assumed to be rational if you are talking to someone in a recognizable language. A frequent public embarrassment is being caught mumbling gibberish even when it merely means you are buried in deep thought. Nor does it help to use recognizable words. Even though you insist on speaking only to intelligent persons and you regard yourself as the most intelligent person you know, you cannot get away with talking to yourself in public.

The result is that all of us are careful to prevent embarrassment by keeping our lips together so sounds of words or other grunts do not escape, or else we must give an account of words we address to ourselves. We can for example, make it clear we are not talking to ourselves but are praying. Sociolinguist Ronald Wardhaugh in an analysis of conversation reminds us that you can talk to your dog but:

. . .only about suitable topics for dog talk—not, for example, about nuclear physics, except perhaps jokingly.

You can also get away with what sociologist Erving Goffman called "response cries," such as "brr" when it's cold, "oops" when you nearly lose your balance, "eek" when you're faced with a minor danger and "yech" on unwrapping a rotting fish. These cries are not entirely addressed to yourself since anyone in your hearing can interpret them as a message.

But you can't address whole sentences to yourself as you walk down the street even if what you say is deeply philosophical and worth listening to. The same goes for what hearers interpret as meaningless. You can only talk nonsense to an audience if you first get a Ph. D. and confine your remarks to helpless students in a lecture hall. Even students have limits to what they will put up with as I learned in my own experience as a professor.

PREVENTING EMBARRASSMENT BY LEARNING TO BE RATIONAL

What about children? Don't they often talk to themselves or with imaginary playmates?

Of course they do with the result that one of the tasks of education is teaching children the difference between fantasy and reality and what is more, the embarrassment and worse they will suffer later if they go on talking to themselves or doing other irrational things.

Sociologist Thomas J. Scheff quotes research which shows that children from age eight on already show a high level of sophistication about details of mental illness. Some play at "acting crazy," mumbling incoherencies, acting confused, or claiming to be goblins or other mythical creatures.

Those same children seem to have no difficulty distinguishing those fantasies from everyday reality. Partly this appears to be a matter of maturation. Some parents and teachers do their part to discourage fantastic thought, even in play.

One way, especially in school, is to jog the child to avoid drifting into reverie. Teachers will direct students to "stop daydreaming!," "sit up straight," or "look at me when I'm talking to you!"

It is not enough for the child merely to act rationally, say by solving problems correctly, answering questions in class and the like. Besides acting rationally children have to look like they're being rational at all times so as to reassure the teacher. We observe children in class at their desks, as they work on an assignment, tighten the muscles of their forehead, narrow their eyes, purse their lips, look upward, bend their heads down till they are practically touching the paper, wrinkle their brows, stroke their chins, scratch their heads and the charming habit of beginners of showing intense concentration by projecting the tip of the tongue out of the side of their mouths.

Many of these same gestures persist into adulthood. Are they learned or genetically programmed? We do not know. But they are important ways of preventing the embarrassment you would otherwise feel if persons you are talking with suspect you are not listening. It is not enough to pay attention. You have to show it.

STREET BEHAVIOR

After persons have learned how to act and look rational, they are now free to walk the street. There a whole new set of behaviors is called for of which the key to acting rational seems to be to act as if you are *going* toward some goal and are moving along at a *pace* likely to get you there.

In spite of the growth of civil rights protection of street people, most persons frown on loitering or lolling. What seems to be at work is our general discomfort at the behavior of persons who do not appear to have any clear goal. For example sociologists Janey Levine, Ann Vinson and Deborah Wood observed persons' choice of seatmates on New York and Boston subways. The most preferred were persons holding books or newspapers who were clearly reading. Least preferred were persons "sprawled in their seats and looking as if they were not going anywhere."

This demand for goal-focused activity means we will only accept a person who is lying down if the person is not merely lying there, but is, for example, "getting a tan" and does so at a place proper for getting a tan. To get license to stare into space, you have to go into a restaurant and first order a cup of coffee. Then you are free to appear to be thinking deeply. Even a street beggar must be careful to stay awake and do some begging.

When it comes to walking down a city street, a whole set of requirements come into play for persons to show they are going somewhere. Just as cars have to keep up to freeway speed, pedestrians have to keep roughly up to the average speed of other pedestrians. If in a hurry, you may walk rapidly but not run unless you're trying to catch a bus, and even then, only for short distances. Through it all you have to weave your way skillfully through the crowd apologizing even for lightly brushing against others, let alone collisions.

102

MAKING YOUR WAY THROUGH
PEDESTRIAN TRAFFIC

There is more to making your way than just avoiding collisions. One sociological report by sociologist Michael Wolff examined persons simply walking down the street in New York City. He found that there was a definite norm on how you are to walk behind someone else. Up to about 10 feet behind another person, you may walk directly behind the person without attracting attention. But if you move any closer you must move slightly to the side so that you are not directly behind. Persons were found to be quite nervous when someone was within 10 feet directly behind them. They would begin looking over their shoulders to the right or left.

Another practice was that of watching the faces of those coming toward them for any signs of alarm. If such occurred, this meant something dangerous or unpredictable was happening behind. This lead the person to turn around to see. In effect persons used those approaching them as a sort of rear-view mirror.

Sociologist Erving Goffman invented the term "civil inattention" to cover a practice in which we all constantly engage without thinking. When we approach others, we glance at them enough to show we know they are there but then we immediately avert our glance to show we have no reason to suspect the other of not having every proper reason to be there, as we ourselves do also. He writes:

> Where this courtesy is performed between two persons passing on the street, civil inattention may take the special form of eyeing the other up to approximately eight feet, during which time sides of the street are apportioned by gesture, and

103

then casting the eyes down as the other passes—a kind of dimming of lights.

He goes on to warn that giving those glances must be done briefly and in a routine manner. If your gaze is guarded, overly dramatic or darts back and forth erratically as if you have something to fear, it can be seen by others as symptomatic of mental disturbance. On the other hand, a common embarrassment is not withdrawing your glance quickly enough and being "caught staring," which also occurs in closed settings such as restaurants or house parties.

Ethologist David Givens found persons in public places to give off strong signals to ward off possible approaches by strangers. He observed persons in Seattle, Washington at a famous local public market, at an Irish bar, and on the campus of the University of Washington. In all three settings, persons approaching strangers whom they could not easily avoid passing near would:

1. press their lips tightly together, bite the lower lip with their upper teeth, slightly protrude the tongue, or press it visibly against the inside of the cheek. Other studies show these to be signs of "social aversiveness." In plain language, they are saying: "Stay away. I want no contact."

2. avert their gaze, often turning the whole head to one side.

3. automanipulate, e.g., touch the face or neck, preen the hair, adjust glasses, put the hand to the nose, cover the mouth or scratch the head. Such gestures have been shown to indicate an indisposition to bond and rejection of any social overtures.

Givens points out that this sort of behavior has been observed among children in nursery school and often in some species of animal primates, suggesting some of these gestures may be genetically coded possibly for protection.

At the same time, persons who fail to lip-bite, avert their gaze or cover their mouth when passing by in public places are setting themselves up for possible unwelcome approaches. They then can become flustered as they try to excuse themselves from their embarrassment at giving off the wrong signals. That means that being careful to lip-bite and so forth helps prevent embarrassments from occurring in the first place.

COMPETENCY AND ATTENTION NORMS

In addition to the kinds of public behavior we have been talking about, there are more general kinds of ways we are all expected to engage in. When we do not, we can easily get embarrassed.

First is general competence. You are expected to be able to maintain your balance with no difficulty as you leap gracefully to oneside or suddenly alter directions if an unexpected obstacle appears. You are presumed to be able to show effortless ease in small tasks such as lighting a cigarette, putting the proper fare into the bus fare-box, or steering your car. You are assumed to be able to mobilize your strength at any moment, to look as though you are in full control of all of your body, your clothes, your bicycle, your pen or anything else you use.

In someone else's company, you are expected to show appropriate attention which means neither drifting off dreamily nor obviously stifling a yawn, nor over-rigid attention or involvement. Several cases brought to my attention deal with social parties in which a couple became over-involved with each other. Two men or two women might find both shared a fascinating interest and proceed to spend much of the evening talking about it. Everyone else was left feeling vaguely uncomfortable and somewhat left out. They also felt a bit embarrassed for the host who kept going over to the two and asking if they "needed anything" when it was obvious that the host was desperately trying to save the party from what he felt was a discourteous distraction.

GLOSSES

"Glosses" are another ingenious observation of sociologist Erving Goffman. He refers here to signs that a person gives off to communicate to all who might care that he or she not only has every right to be there but can be depended on to behave properly.

Here are some examples he gives. If you are in an airport waiting lounge and find the only vacant seat occupied by someone's travelling case, you will hesitate to remove it. But if you do you will find you head off possible embarrassment, should the owner suddenly appear, if you remove it by the very tips of your fingers as if being careful not to pollute it by too forthright or solid a grasp.

Sometimes persons overplay a gesture to show they are properly mannered persons deserving of acceptance. When a car stops to allow a pedestrian the right of way the pedestrian may affect a slight running stance even though he or she is really not moving any faster.

A person who must leave a public meeting early will exaggerate his movements as he tip-toes out of the room, often crouched over so far as to actually attract more attention to himself than if he simply walked to the door in normal stature.

There we see the point: the gesture has the effect, however unconscious, of attracting attention by its sheer exaggeration. This does not mean the person does it to attract attention. He really means not to disturb but employs a gesture well know to those in the room. The gesture proclaims:

> I am aware I might be thought rude. I have pressing business elsewhere. Please forgive me. Look how I abase myself. I am almost crawling out of here. So don't stop anything. Go right on with the meeting.

If you employ this gesture, you *are* forgiven and need feel little embarrassment. Others are bothered much less than you think. I discovered this when I crept out of a meeting, then apologized later to some who I am sure watched me leave. They were puzzled, saying they did not realize I had left early.

ORGANIZED PREVENTATIVES

A few persons are lucky enough to be able to call on organizational resources to prevent embarrassment. In her studies of a large corporation sociologist Rosabeth Moss Kanter reports on how executive secretaries help present a "front for their bosses." The boss can be protected from being embarrassed by unexpected visitors who might otherwise observe the boss in his or her office practicing golf putting shots. Often such executives in government have spokespersons to "explain" what the executive rally meant when he or she misspoke at a public meeting.

Humbler examples are presented by wives of alcoholics who explain their husbands' absence from work as due to "nerves" or "pressure." Sociologist Charlotte Green Schwartz has examined the ways in which wives of mentally ill men try to explain away symptoms by insisting that he just has "little peculiarities like the rest of us." Should he resist going to a psychiatrist the wife may tell her husband that it is she who needs psychiatric care and ask her husband to accompany her. The shift can be made later or handled by family therapy.

PREPARATION

I have been describing different ways embarrassment is prevented, sometimes deliberately, sometimes by the training we had in growing up. In the end the simplest way is to prepare carefully for any situation you can anticipate that may cause embarrassment. Persons can be trained in finishing schools and public speaking classes and important occasions such as weddings can of course be rehearsed.

Prepartion means observing any situation you are about to enter carefully. For instance, if you have to give a speech, you can make a checklist such as the following:

If possible, inspect the hall carefully ahead of time
Decide where you will sit, if there's a choice. If it is unclear, ask your host ahead of time.
Are there microphone cords to trip on?
Is there a step up to the platform?
Is the microphone the right height for you?
If your speech is written out, make a photocopy should the original be thrown out with the trash.

Is there a lectern for your notes and you need one, ask for one. The host is glad to help since his reputation is also on the line.

For other occasions you can do the same. Look around and ask what could go wrong. Look yourself over as well. If you wear a wig and the net has a string for tightening, you can stop at a mirror to check that the string is not hanging out. Otherwise someone may seek to do you a favor by reaching over to remove the string.

Above all, beware of zippers! Art Linkletter writes of a man who went to a movie after a heavy dinner, relaxing in his seat by loosening his zipper, as many do. He jumped up to let a woman push by to get the seat next to his. In the process he hurriedly zipped up his pants catching a part of her dress in his zipper. As each tried to move they became conscious of what had happened. After a few tugs the two of them had to sidle out together and waddle up the aisle to the lobby, all the while providing more entertainment for the audience than the film was offering.

For such embarrassment, the most general preventative of all is: GO SLOWLY. I made a rough count of the embarrassments I have run across and concluded that about one in three could have been prevented if the persons involved had slowed down to half-speed.

Of course slowing down has its own costs not the least being the reputation many of us like to think we have for being agile, fast on the uptake, clever and sharp. Even if we slow down, there remain all the embarrassments that occur anyhow. What then? It is often still possible to hide the embarrassment or ignore it. Let's look at some ways of doing so in the next chapter.

Chapter 7

Hiding and Pretending:
Can They Work?

There is really no question that we try to hide when we feel embarrassed. We lower our heads, avert our eyes, cover our faces and even try to escape from the scene altogether.

How far we go in hiding was shown in a study of the long running TV series, CANDID CAMERA by sociologists Thomas J. Scheff and Suzanne M. Retzinger. In the series, persons were tricked by a set-up. For example persons would face what was apparently a talking mailbox. In a famous scene the motor of a car was removed beforehand and the car coasted down a hill into a garage. The driver then innocently asked the mechanic why the car would not start. In each case the target persons' reactions would be caught by a hidden camera including their expressions when they were told they had been fooled.

The researchers collected 254 consecutive episodes and had raters carefully classify and count gestures and comments. Although it was not surprising for these persons to show embarrassment, what is interesting is how far they went in trying to hide. Here are some findings:

Gesture	Percentage
One or both hands over face, eyes or mouth	48%
Hands touching face, hair, neck or chest	44%
Head down or turned to one side or head and body turned around	73%

In addition eleven percent tried to run away and two percent tried to hide behind the furniture.

Many would display more than one of these gestures. For example in one situation, the host, Allan Funt, pretended to be a camera clerk who implied that her photographs were pornographic. After protests from the customer and a demand to see the manager, Funt revealed who he was. Scheff and Retzinger describe her reaction:

> As she turned away, laughing, she covered her face with one hand...She said, "Oh my God," turned toward (Funt), and hid her face in his shoulder. As she turned to escape (a second time, she touched her hair and face, with her eyes closed. She went through this cycle. . .several times. . .All told, she displayed hiding gestures twenty-two times, more than one every two seconds.

Her reactions were far from uncommon.

CAN YOU KEEP YOUR HIDING SECRET?

In the CANDID CAMERA episodes persons are trying to hide but the camera reveals those attempts. Can people get away with hiding when there is no camera around?

The answer is that frequently hiding does work. Sometimes you can hurry to the bathroom to clean off a stain on your blouse before anyone notices. Embarrassing tattoos may be covered over by a skilled tattooist. Drug needle markings can be protected from public view with long sleeved shirts and by being careful to shower when there are no witnesses.

Lawrence Langner in a book aptly titled The *Importance of Wearing Clothes* claims that clothes may conceal erections experienced by men in the presence of other men's wives. Clothes may also hide the pubic hair and budding breasts of young girls protecting them from premature sexual advances. Although it seems dubious that clothes necessarily have those effects (witness the lack of arousal described by anthropologists and observers in societies where both sexes wear few clothes), there is no question that clothing does change appearance.

Reports of females who put on men's attire to fight in the United States Civil War provide evidence that concealment even under extreme conditions of close living can succeed. Loreta Janeta Velazquez, a woman of Cuban birth who sought to join the Confederacy partly to be near her husband but partly out of an attraction to battle itself was able to develop a totally effective disguise by liberal use of padding and binding. Under her assumed name of Lieutenant Harry T. Buford she succeeded in recruiting a battalion of 236 men. Her problem was not her costume but rather having to resist the occasional overtures to her from women who could hardly resist so attractive a "man".

Less heroic but just as important to those doing it are attempts of college students to conceal marks on examinations. In a study of students at a large provincial university in Western Canada, sociologists Daniel and Cheryl Albas found that students who did exceptionally well on examinations were called "Aces" in contrast to those who did poorly who were called "Bombers."

While Aces often bragged to other Aces about their scores, they were much more circumspect with others whose downcast faces suggested they were Bombers. To them Aces would avoid revealing their own scores preferring to help save the face of the Bombers by talking about how unfair certain questions were.

Bombers were much more aggressive in concealing their scores. Some were quick to fold the paper over or stuff it immediately into their binders. If the test was handed back at the close of the hour, Bombers would, after a quick glance at their mark, make a show of rushing out of the room as if in a hurry for an urgent appointment.

Persons who anticipated doing poorly might follow the example of the following student:

> If I know I did poorly on the test...I plan to 'accidentally' be away from...class. This way I can prevent others from knowing my mark and so save myself a lot of pain and, embarrassment. Later I go to the professor's office and pick up my paper when none of my classmates are around.

This student is trading facing his classmates for facing his professor which may be even more embarrassing. But he may be able to cover with a proper expression of contriteness and a request for a chance to do extra work to make up for the poor grade. This has its own risks, as I can tell you from personal experience, since students may do even more poorly on the extra work thus affirming the correctness of the earlier grade.

WHAT CAN BE CONCEALED?

The possibility of trying to hide embarrassing facts or features varies enormously. Incipient AIDS or a family breakup may be slow in developing and not be revealed until far along. A speech defect on the other hand will be revealed the moment the person utters his or her first words. Persons making appointments for job interviews by phone may quite unintentionally fail to reveal gender or race leading to later embarrassments on personal confrontation.

A man seeking a place to sit at a crowded restaurant may ask a lone woman seated at a large table if she minds if he shares the table. After she agrees and they later get ready to leave, the man may be suddenly thrown when the woman asks him to please get her wheelchair which is parked next to the wall nearby. Often his being flustered is revealed in valiant gestures as in a gallant offer to call her a taxi. She then has to inform him that she has her handicapped equipped car parked near the door. He is left feeling vaguely dissatisfied as he mutters that he did not know or that he is sorry and she hastens to assure him that "It's alright and thank you". It is not easy to get gracefully out of such situations minor as they are.

The result is that as sociologist Erving Goffman, who wrote a whole book on stigmas, points out some embarrassing stigmas may be visible to one group and invisible to another. Prostitutes, thieves and drug addicts are very careful in not exposing themselves to the police but they cannot avoid exposing themselves to the point of advertisement to clients, fences and some of their own as in the following report from a call girl:

> I always look around a room fast when I go to parties... You never know. Once I ran smack into two of my cousins. They were a couple of call girls and didn't even nod to me. I took my cue—hoping they were too busy thinking of themselves to wonder about me. I always wondered what I would do if I ran into my father, since he was around quite a bit.

Sometimes persons who are not trying to hide anything may become irritated by well-meaning efforts of others to "protect" them. For example, a visually impaired person may detect others are censoring their speech by being careful to avoid expressions such as " I see," or any reference of the latest movies.

The person may become so conscious of such efforts that they suspect others of such censorship even when none is occurring. The result can make interaction so painful that persons find themselves simply avoiding each other using socially acceptable excuses.

In an attempt to avoid such problems, persons may try to make things easier for the others by a process that sociologists Joseph W. Schneider and Peter Conrad call "preventive telling." They interviewed a sample of 80 persons with epilepsy. In spite of the availability of effective treatments and medication, and even though most persons are aware that epilepsy is a disease, the investigators report that epileptics continue to face discrimination in some types of employment and buying insurance. Survey data have shown that objections to employing epileptics are registered by 18% of the population in former West Germany, by 11% in Italy, by 9% in the United States and by 7% in Denmark. In addition many persons become quite frightened when they actually witness an epileptic seizure. Persons may become panicky because they do not know whom to call or whether the person may hurt him or herself.

Knowing of these feelings, epileptics may tell trusted others so they will know what to expect and not be frightened. One of Schneider and Conrad's subjects said:

> Down the road, I'll usually make a point to tell someone I'm around a lot because I know that it's frightening. So I will. . .tell them I've got it; if I have one (seizure) that it's nothing to worry about. And don't take me to the hospital even if I ask you to. I always tell people that I work with because I presume - I'll be with them for some long period of time.

Others said they do such "preventive telling" as a way of testing friendship so as to minimize the pain of later rejection. In the words of one:

> Why go through all the trauma of falling in love with someone if they are going to hate your guts once they find out you're an epileptic?

PERSONAL NAMES

Persons change their names for many reasons. Some changes announce a change of identity as when a newly ratified member of a monastery or convent is assigned a new name. Some change their names for self-protection as in criminal aliases. An accountant may think it prudent to publish his racy novel under a pen name.

The courts are liberal in allowing name changes unless the petitioner is doing so for fraudulent reasons, to escape legitimate debts or to evade local laws. For example, in Garden Grove, California, a local ordinance prohibited candidates from stating a political position in their ballot designation. An attempt by a city councilman running for mayor to change his name from Robert Dinsen to "Robert Frank Tax fighter Bob Dinsen" was denied by the court.

Such attempts are rare. In a study of petitioners for a legal name change in Los Angeles County, sociologists Leonard Broom, Helen B. Beem and Virginia Harris report that changes were likely to be allowed when, for example:

> ...the surname of a divorcee (is) a source of embarrassment because it implies an obsolete relationship.

117

Others change their names because they have obscene or humorous connotations. King County, Washington Superior Court Judge Richard Ishikawa told of a couple named "Schitz" who had:

> ...been kidded all their lives about it and they just didn't want their kids to go through it too.

Some names simply appear funny to children who can be very cruel. A woman reported to researcher Mary C. Waters that children she grew up with who had complicated Italian names were made fun of by other children:

> I had a girlfriend, her last name was Polilissio. That made the kids hysterical.

Although sorry for her girlfriend, the woman says she was glad she could herself "pass" as non-Italian since her grandfather dropped the "i" from the family name of "Alberti."

Ethnic identifications may be concealed and then proudly revealed by later generations. The founder of the Guggenheim dynasty was a Jew named Simon who married Rachel. Their grandsons were named Daniel, Solomon and Benjamin, recognizably Biblical if not Jewish. With intermarriage and style changes, later generations were named Jean, Jack, Betty, Terrence and Willard.

Young Jewish couples now are rediscovering roots with the restoration of Biblical or straightforward Hebrew names such as Yitzchak (for Isaac) and Rivkah (for Rachel). So too African Americans adopt African names or prefer names that make religion clear as when Cassius Clay, the boxer, became Mohammed Ali.

Such cases belong in this book for they make clear that persons can totally reject any sense of embarrassment if they feel strongly enough about their identity to be proud of it. A final case shows that neither embarrassment nor pride need interfere with one's business sense. When famed opera soprano Maria Callas was interviewed at the New York Metropolitan Opera House, the reporter asked:

> You were born in the United States, you were brought up in Greece, you are now practically an Italian. What language do you think in?

Miss Callas, perhaps thinking of upcoming negotiations with the Metropolitan, replied:

> I count in English.

NAMES OF OCCUPATIONS

When persons are embarrassed by the kind of work they do they will often try to keep it secret. Sometimes members of an occupation may act together and try to upgrade the work by changing its name altogether to one in which they can take pride.

In that way hairdressers become beauticians, bartenders are taught their trade in a College of Mixology and scrap iron dealers insist that they are "salvage specialists." In a classic restaurant study in Chicago, sociologist William F. Whyte tells us that the various foods had different statuses along which went pay differences in spite of small or nonexistent skill differences.

Those who worked on the range were at the top of this status world with the following in decreasing status order: salad sta-

119

tion, chicken and meat preparation, chicken cooking and vegetable preparation. At the very bottom was the fish station. This upset the supervisor who was the target of a string of often amusing remarks from others who saw her as polluted by contact with smelly and dirty work. She complained bitterly to the interviewer who she thought was writing a book:

> (Staff) go by and say, 'There's the fish lady'...One thing you must remember in your book. You must not call this the fish station. This is the sea-food station. Yes, that's the name it should have.

Attempts to cover up undesirable connotations of names extends to diseases or disabilities. In spite of modern sophistication about medicine, persons continue to fear some diseases or disabilities especially if they think others will be frightened or embarrassed. An epileptic may insist he has occasional "fainting spells" while persons with hearing difficulties will avoid the words "hard of hearing" in favor of "hearing impaired." Some alcoholics, even if recovering, may still lay claim to "enjoying a social drink before dinner," persons formerly labeled under "Mongolism" are recorded as showing "Down's Syndrome" and hyperactive children are designated as persons with "attention deficits." I recognize that some of these newer names are intended to be more precise or to conform more closely to psychiatric diagnoses. Still the names do help remove some of the unfortunate embarrassing stigma that older names often conveyed.

BODY FUNCTIONS

The most striking cases of name changing are the euphemisms or softened expressions that surround body functions. Although we are getting a little more permissive, we still have far to go to get back to the Middle Ages when words such as "shit," "piss", "vomit" and "snot" were used without much concern. Dan Sabbath and Mandel Hall (themselves pseudonyms) in their book entitled *End Product* tell us:

> First the spelling changed to "s—t." Then the word disappeared from respectable literature altogether. Before 1700 we might have had to "perform the work of nature" or "evacuate." After that date, the poetry of evasion blossomed. We could do a job, pay a call, make a visit, wash our hands. The women might pluck a rose, pick a daisy, go see auntie, or powder the nose.

The toilet itself became the privy, the gong, the siege-hole or boggard. In anti-establishment originality, it was also called the house of office, the necessary vault, the draught chapel, the chapel of ease and the throne room.

In our time we have the john, lavatory, W. C. (for water closet), bathroom, washroom, and little boys or girls room. In a visit to St. Francisville, Mississippi, I saw that the toilets in a tourist center were each labeled "Necessary Room." Although this was intended to convey a slight flavor of antebellum manners, modern tour guides will usually be careful to point to what they call "the conveniences."

All this embarrassment about normal body functions raises the question as to why there is such concern. It appears to be very widespread among all social classes and is certainly not confined to the United States. Why should that be? It turns out to be tied up with beliefs we have that certain things should always be kept hidden because they are private. We are taught to be embarrassed about them as a way of reminding us to keep them private.

PRIVACY OF PERSONAL ACTS

Consider these three activities: *sex, defecation and urination.* Although very different from one another, these activities are practically always carried out in private. They are also monumental sources of embarrassment when not carried out in private or revealed publicly. For instance persons will try to disattend to sounds of sexual arousal that penetrate narrow apartment house walls or feel embarrassed when sounds of a flushing toilet are overheard by your dinner guests. Persons may be horrified at remnants of body excreta left on clothing and hurry to hide them or change clothes at the first opportunity .

All of these activities are certainly not shameful. They are all natural but are embarrassing all the same. Sex for example is nothing to be ashamed of, even a mark of a "healthy animal." Yet even in nudist camps persons do not perform sex openly in front of others. In so-called "swinging parties" where persons exchange sexual partners, the evidence is that those are very private occasions to which only a select few are invited who can be counted on to behave themselves. The same goes for staged shows which are just that rather than the real thing as well as peep-hole arrangements in brothels where the customer at least believes he is in private.

It is true that in France, Japan and several other countries, men may urinate behind scarcely concealed partitions or even casually in a half hidden alleyway between two buildings. But they still do so in a circumspect manner being careful to conceal the penis or at least cover it if only by the hand. Even in those countries women are not allowed the same license, a fact which involves more than a matter of sexism as we shall see. So too at group or mass physical examinations as in armed services inductions, persons are careful to avert their eyes, maintaining civil inattention, allowing each other at least an illusion of privacy. Why do they not simply stare openly?

WHY REVELATION OF PERSONAL ACTS IS EMBARRASSING

Sociologist Barrington Moore, Jr., in a detailed study of privacy, presents data from classical Athens, ancient China, the Old Testament, and from a review of anthropological studies of many societies. He concludes that, when it comes to sex and elimination, there seems to be a near-universal feeling that those acts must be carried out if not in privacy then at least not in a totally unconcerned manner in the presence of others. The fact that this feeling is found so widely leads us to suspect that there may be something genetic about it. That suspicion is supported by the discovery that not only human but many animals, especially the primates, also carry out sex and elimination in private if it is possible.

If something is built into our genetic makeup, we have to ask what survival value it has. For instance, among many animals, females mate only with a dominant male leaving the other males permanently frustrated except for a quickie when the dominant is not looking. The explanation is that the dominant is usually stronger and monopolizes the food supply as well as the best sleeping and dwelling places. He therefore offers the best chance that the female's offspring will be strong, healthy and well-cared for to maturity. With such offspring, the future of the species is better assured than if the female mated with weaker males.

What then is the survival value of carrying on sex and elimination in private? Biologically speaking, they have in common that they require intense concentration on the task at hand. Copulation, urination and defecation represent imperious demands which, in Barrington Moore, Jr.'s words:

> ...go through a specifiable series of physiological states to culminate in a strong sensation of relief or joy.

There is something else as well. All three of these personal activities do not admit of interruption without distress. Once you start, you have to keep going or the whole thing may fail.

But how could all this help our remote ancestors to survive? The fact that they all require us to be self-absorbed is precisely the problem. For while focused on bringing it off, we are in a highly vulnerable position. In our remote pre-ancestry, an enemy sneaking up for an attack would find that the best time to pounce would be while we are defecating, urinating or copulating.

We can, then, speculate that those early humans who made sure they carried out those things in private were less likely to be pounced upon and therefore survived to hand on their genes to their offspring. Others are just not here to offer an exception to this claim .

We have here a possible answer to why men are usually allowed to be somewhat more casual than women about urinating, men being often permitted to use any semi-hidden spot while women require an enclosed place. If suddenly threatened a man *can* interrupt quickly and move away but women, having to assume a squat position, are more vulnerable for the simple reason that they have to get up if surprised.

Of course all these claims about the survival value of events that happened many thousands of years ago is speculative. The argument is not entirely fanciful even in modern times. Biographer Leon C. Metz writes of the death of Pat Garrett, the lawman who had killed the outlaw, Billy the Kid. Accompanied by others riding nearby, Garrett was riding in a buggy with a friend in an isolated part of the Territory of New Mexico in 1908 when the driver stopped to let himself and Garrett urinate. Garrett stood with his shotgun in his right hand while he unbuttoned his trousers with his left. Shortly thereafter a bullet ripped into the back of his neck. Perhaps because Billy the Kid had become a local folk hero, no one was ever convicted of the murder.

WHY WE STILL GET EMBARRASSED

Even if those who got embarrassed about copulation and elimination were the ones more likely to survive, why are these matters still embarrassing when the danger of being attacked is mostly gone? Why do we continue to teach our children to maintain privacy by the methods that parents seem to use everywhere, such as:

> For goodness sake, close the toilet door!
> Look what a mess you made of your pants. Try to be more careful!
> Look at the way he's pawing her! You'd think they'd know better in public.

Quite apart from evolutionary pressures, there is another reason we continue to carry out these activities in private. While doing them, we are *so carried away that we cannot control the image of ourselves* that we normally project.

Back in Chapter 2 we found that we get embarrassed when our identity is inappropriate or discredited. But when we are self-absorbed, we cannot pay any attention to presenting an appropriate identity. We then may do things that are terribly embarrassing if anyone sees them.

One correspondent wrote me as follows:

> Two years ago when my husband and I started dating, we were in the foreplay stage of lovemaking when he reached down to the back of my ass and found toilet paper stuck between my "cheeks" from some hours before. If the lights had been on he would have seen my red face—I could have died. He took it really well but I'll never forget it.

So too with urination and defecation. While doing them, we are too self-absorbed to control how others may think of us. We protect ourselves by locking doors and pulling curtains over windows. We also assume others will be careful to avoid embarrassing us and themselves by staying clear and, if that fails, then at least by eye aversion.

IS HIDING BEING DISHONEST?

I have brought up sex and elimination because they make it clear that hiding is not always a matter of being dishonest. As we have shown, there are good reasons why life in society is more pleasant because we carry out those activities hidden from public view.

There are others which are not so easily defensible such as hiding one's ethnic origins in a name change or trying to deceive by hiding wrinkles under an ascot scarf. Here we encounter modern pressure on all of us to be honest and authentic.

There is furthermore, a real danger that a person's cover may be blown. Covering a stain on the apartment wall with a picture runs the risk that the string holding the picture will wear through at an unpredictable moment. Or consider the following experience of a woman at a cocktail party in which persons were standing around in clusters in animated talk:

> I was wearing a ring which had several prongs holding the jewels in place. I spotted a friend and waved to her just as a man was brushing by me. Unfortunately my ring caught his hairpiece and whisked it off leaving it hooked on my ring. For the moment I wasn't sure what had happened and tried desperately to shake it loose. The man turned to me and said drily: "May I help? I think that's mine." That's all anyone remembered about the party for years.

The man is revealed not simply as wearing the hairpiece but, if he had kept it secret, of trying to conceal that fact. Still many persons do conceal embarrassing facts and get away with it.

Then there are some which cannot be concealed. One historic case involved the man later to become the third United States president, Thomas Jefferson when in 1786 he was serving as minister to France. A widower then aged 43, he had a love affair with a married woman named Maria Cosway. Although such liaisons were tacitly condoned in those days, his apparently resulted in his fracturing his right wrist.

Although there is controversy over what happened, historian Dumas Malone writes in his monumental six volume work on Jefferson that the temptation to associate the accident with Mrs. Cosway is "irresistible." Historian Charles van Pelt records one story which held that Jefferson had tried to leap over a fence preparatory to helping Mrs. Cosway get across. Another a bit less romantic but perhaps more likely is that as he rushed out of his home to meet her, he fell as he jumped over an ornamental pool. He fractured his wrist in trying to brake his fall.

Jefferson was his usual reticent self. He wrote to a friend shortly after the incident:

> How the right hand became disabled would be a long story for the left to tell.

The left never did tell but the fact of the wrist injury which caused him pain and discomfort for the rest of his life could hardly be concealed. A modern investigative reporter would not have left the story where Jefferson did. I cannot help but feel that what was bothering Jefferson was not that the love affair would be more widely known but that he, playing the dapper lover, was not able to make it over the fence or the pool.

Jefferson's general reputation was of course a major protection for his efforts to hide the cause if not the effect. The rest of us have to live with the problems of concealment. Sometimes we can hide our embarrassments and it may even be desirable. But sometimes we cannot and we do not have Jefferson's resources. What then? That is what we turn to next.

PART III

Managing
Embarrassment

Suppose all efforts to prevent or hide your embarrassment fail or are inappropriate. What do you do then?

Many of us then fumble to excuse what happened, try to justify what we did, seek for some kind of account or just apologize. Some research has been done on these devices starting with a famous analysis by British philosopher John Austin in a classic essay: "A Plea for Excuses." I think it is useful to start by looking at embarrassments and ask what sort of strategies seem most useful for handling them. Some call for excuses and other accounts. But some call for action when words do not help much.

For embarrassments, four basic strategies seem to work best, each of them the topic of one of the next four chapters. Here they are.

1. You can try to *reduce or deny the significance* of the event. After all you can claim, there is no need to get upset.

2. You can *change its meaning* or reinterpret the event. It is really not so bad as it looks.

3. You can *transform your identity*. It was not you or not the real you.

4. You can make a *social move*. You ask for help, seek to repair the damage or involve other people.

Here are some examples.

When you try to *reduce its significance*, you claim the embarrassing incident is not really important. For instance after you and your partner make your way to your seats in a movie house, you reach into what you thought was your partner's box of popcorn only to find it belongs to a total stranger. In one case reported to me, the person felt so embarrassed that he offered to buy the other person another box of popcorn. The other not only refused but encourged him to help himself to more popcorn!

There are many ways of *changing the meaning* of the event. For instance in the summer of 1938, Douglas G. Corrigan set out in his single-engine plane to fly west to Los Angeles but ended up in Ireland. He offered no explanation other than to say: "I guess I went the wrong way." He earned for himself the name of Wrong-Way Corrigan and at least a footnote in aviation history. His event was changed in meaning from a stupid move to an historical anecdote.

Some people positively glory in their flubs. Former Baseball pitcher Dizzy Dean would, when announcing a game, tell us that the player "slud into third." A worthy successor is former catcher Yogi Berra who on being honored in St. Louis told the crowd:

I want to thank all the people who made this night necessary.

What might simply be a wildly confused embarrassment was converted by Berra's word magic into a marvelous anecdote. Although we can rarely come up with word magic ourselves, there are many ways of changing the interpretation of what would otherwise be an embarrassment .

A different strategy is *changing your identity* in some way so that your embarrassment is now appropriate or explainable.

Something like that happened to former President Gerald Ford when he fell down some steps, bumped his head getting out of a plane and tripped at another time. Since he had been a famous athlete yet showed he could be a good sport about these incidents in the face of stories told by night-club comedians, he gained a reputation as a very human person who could own up to his deficiencies.

Often it is obvious that the persons did not mean it. During the Israel War of Independence in 1948, when Israelis and Arabs were locked in combat, Ambassador to the United Nations Warren Austin pleaded with them to "resolve their differences like good Christians." The ambassador was clearly so overburdened with affairs of state that he was not quite himself.

Finally there is the strategy of making a *social move*. Here you try to shift the responsibity onto others, involve them in some way in your response or depend on others for help. Sometimes you are saved by others in unexpected ways. In the days when milk was still delivered door to door, a woman mixed up a love note she had meant to stuff into her husband's lunch box with her order for milk to the milkman. To her surprise she got a note back from the milkman saying:

> Since you feel that way about me, I've left an extra quart
> of milk for your husband. It sounds like he needs it.

It took some explaining to her husband yet made a great story to tell her friends.

In other situations you can assume that others will protect you by not looking or explaining for you until you can recover your aplomb. You have to be able to anticipate when this is appropriate and when it is not.

Let us look at how the four strategies work.

Chapter 8

Reducing Significance

When you get embarrassed your concern is that some damage may be done to your image or to the situation. If you can show that no such thing has really happened, then that solves the problem and there is no need to feel embarrassed at all.

Often simply laughing and plunging right ahead will do it. A laugh, especially when others join in, is a way of saying that the whole incident is not to be taken seriously.

SHOULD YOU TRY FOR A CLEVER COMMENT?

The answer to that is easy. Yes, if the reply is funny and if you can take credit for it. The only danger is that if you are too original or clever you are seen as a showoff. The comment draws attention to yourself when what you are trying to do is to make light of the embarrassment and move on. Sometimes others even suspect you may have deliberately brought on the embarrassment so you could come up with the delicious saying that shows how brilliant you are.

Still there are clever comments which are so well-put that they are fun to read about, if not to use. Usually they are attributed to some famous person.

When British conductor Sir Thomas Beecham was rehearsing his orchestra, he called out to the third flute that he was too loud. A musician called back that the third flute had not yet arrived. The unflappable Sir Thomas shot back:

Well, tell him when he gets here.

Writer Dorothy Parker was once invited to a dinner party by the wife of a movie studio executive named Peabody. Mrs. Peabody delivered the invitation in person and after Miss Parker's acceptance, left. Miss Parker turned to her secretary and said:

After a decent interval, write a note to those illiterate, phony bores that I can't make their damned party...

She was interrupted by the sudden appearance of Mrs. Peabody who had overheard the remark. Without pause Miss Parker continued:

...because I'm dining that evening with the Peabodys.

The famous British political leader Winston Churchill was also the master of the *bon-mot* which he often used to devastating effect. In his eighties Churchill revisited the House of Commons. A member disturbed by the commotion his visit was causing remarked to another:

After all, they say he is potty.

They say he can't hear either.

was Churchill's resounding response.

Sometimes the clever reply may be late in coming. During a 1976 TV debate President Gerald Ford assured the audience there was "no Soviet domination of Eastern Europe." The remark was widely laughed at as a blooper since at the time Eastern

Europe *was* so dominated. President Ford had the last laugh when in 1989 democratic changes shook Poland. Ford said:

> I came out pretty well as a prophet.

Lyndon B. Johnson, as vice-president used to complain about the uselessness of the position. But when President John Kennedy sent him on a mission to French President Charles de Gaulle, Johnson was able to add some class to the job.

The General looked down on Johnson and said in a superior manner:

> Now, Mr. Johnson, what have you come to learn from us?

Johnson smiled broadly and replied:

> Why, General, simply everything you can possibly teach me.

Finally, just so we distribute the cleverness to both parties, Abraham Lincoln who was often mocked for his homely face was once called a "two-faced man" by famed debater Stephen A. Douglas. Lincoln said:

> I leave it to my audience. If I had another face do you think I would wear this one?

These stories are amusing to all of us but repeating them is risky since we are never sure the famous person actually said them. Even when the person him or herself insists they did, they sometimes are simply forgetful or are glad to take credit for the saying if it is memorable. On the other hand, Agatha Christie, the mystery writer denies ever having made the following claim. She was married to an archaeologist and was asked what that was like. The best possible husband, she answered.

The older I get, the more interested he is in me.

In spite of her denial, the story persists because it is just too good.

When such stories are told to save someone from embarrassment, we are ready to forgive the teller if the story is good enough. Such was the case with President Reagan's first meeting with Mikhail Gorbachev. After the meeting, Reagan's press secretary, Larry Speakes reported to journalists that the President had said after the meeting:

The world rests easier because we're meeting here today.

Well put. However Mr. Speakes explained later that Reagan had said almost nothing at the time. Mr. Speakes defended his invention by pointing out that with Gorbachev coming up with one liners one after another, Speakes felt he had to protect Reagan from the embarrassment of being outshone by Mr. Gorbachev. In Reagan's defense, it also appears that he had been cautioned not to talk *extempore* because of a tendency to wander.

Most of us do not have to worry about such problems. We do not have the skill nor presence of mind to come up with a clever bit of repartee when we are embarrassed. At least we cannot do so at the time. I remember hearing a definition of "repartee" as what you think of on the way home when it is too late to save the embarrassment. What then can we do?

MAKING LIGHT OF WHAT HAS HAPPENED

What we can do is to show that the flub is simply not important. For instance, speakers who lose their place can simply admit it and when they find it again go right on as if no harm has been done. If they can do this without blushing or feeling that any great wrong has been done, most audiences are quick to forgive or not even notice there has been a break.

If this happens to you but you feel you must comment while searching for your place, you might try for a bit of amusement with:

> I seem to have lost my place—for which some of you may be very grateful.

Or:

> I had some really great thoughts here but they seem to be hidden under some jam fingerprints left there by a certain little boy named Jeremy who's going to get it when I get home.

Most of the time though, the less said the better for that is the best way to make sure the event is accorded little attention.

Many times embarrassment can be passed off as simply an accident which really does not reflect on you. In a crowded bus anyone might bump into anyone. When you are carrying a lot of parcels, one might drop or when hurrying down some steps, anyone might lose their footing for a moment. No comment is necessary.

Sometimes the event itself can be demoted in significance. For instance when you flub your lines in an amateur play, you can excuse it by reminding people that, after all you are all there to have some fun. The same goes for a poorly thought out move in a friendly game of bridge.

Making light of an event is especially relevant to the many embarrassments of teen-agers or of any beginners. Such persons are allowed some degree of license to make a few mistakes without being hanged for them. The new worker is not a bumbler. He or she is expected to do some stupid things. They are only stupid on the part of the old hand.

Because of my interest in embarrassment, I like to take any opportunity to ask famous persons what embarrasses them. On one occasion, the modern artist Roy Lichtenstein was holding a retrospective in Seattle giving me the chance to ask him whether he was ever embarrassed by a showing of his work. He thought for a moment and then replied:

> No, I don't show anything I would find embarrassing. (Then thinking for a moment, he added with a smile) I do find embarrassing some of the stuff I did when I was young. Not that it's so bad but rather I'm embarrassed to think I once thought it was so good.

There are many kinds of beginners. A newly married couple are forgiven their nervousness in public just as children are excused for their continual violations of public norms of behavior. At least this is true up to a point.

Here are some examples of reported embarrassments which are not immediately forgiven but which can be if you try.

TRIPPING IN A PUBLIC PLACE

A lanky young man with no physical disabilities tells of getting on a bus paying his fare and then falling down as he turned to walk down the aisle. This not uncommon experience should be regarded for what it was. It was a minor occurrence which caused no interruption of anything important and was no reflection on his agility or usual command of his body. Buses lurch unpredictably throwing passengers off balance much of the time.

In another case a woman tripped and could not stop several people from inquiring: "Are you O. K.?" even after she clearly did not welcome their repeated expressions of concern.

If you find such experiences too uncomfortable to ignore, it is useful to have something to say both to underline your command of yourself and to reassure everyone that you are O. K. One possibility is to stand up, look around and announce in a firm voice,

> Now that I've got your attention, I don't have my speech ready.

Or perhaps in Peter Sellers Inspector Clouseau fashion, if you are brave enough you might say,

> I see there's nothing of interest on the floor, so I'll take a seat.

COUGHING FIT

A middle aged woman who was attending a noon meeting of a club, was seized with a coughing fit as the speaker was just getting started. When stifling it did not work, she knew she would have to leave the room. But if you do this (as she did), you must be prepared for the fact that people are looking at you and there is naturally some concern. Someone, suspecting you have a chicken bone stuck in your throat, may even grab you in a Heimlich maneuver. That did not happen to this woman but there was a pause by the speaker as he joined in the anxious looks in her direction. She remained embarrassed as she left the room.

If you are confronted with such a situation, you should say something both to relieve their anxiety and to show the matter is of no significance. Between coughs, you might try saying:

> I know some people will do anything to get attention, but I'm usually more eloquent.

Or, addressing the speaker directly:

> Please don't stop for my sake. I'll be right back.

FALLING ON THE STREET AND SPILLING PACKAGES

A man writes of coming out of a supermarket, his arms full of bags of groceries. Suddenly he lost his footing, slipped to a half-kneeling position and in the process the groceries went flying in all directions. Fortunately nothing broke. He was embarrassed as he hurriedly got up, trying to retrieve everything and rush to his car where he would be out of sight.

Such a reaction is the natural one when we are embarrassed. We want to leave the scene as quickly as possible and forget the whole thing. In this case, a useful gesture is to do just the reverse. Instead of getting up from a half-kneeling position, sit down flat on the ground and look around at the groceries in disgust. If any remain in your arms, drop them too. If you are sitting already, then lie down flat on your back, or sideways on one elbow looking disgusted. This gestural display announces to everyone, as clearly as possible, that this is an *accident*, that such things do not normally happen to you and you want everyone to witness this rare event. You will be met with good-natured smiles from others and I bet that people will rush over to help you up. Do not refuse. Let them be helpful. Most people enjoy doing so. In fact they will probably put all your groceries back into the bags for you. They will each have an interesting incident to tell their friends about and you will be revealed as a person who accepted one of life's daily unpredictable events calmly.

DISCOVERING AN UNZIPPED SKIRT OR UNBUTTONED BLOUSE

A young woman wrote of chatting with a man seated next to her at a rock concert when she suddenly noticed that her skirt was unzipped revealing her pink slip. Another woman wrote of a similar experience with her blouse discovering it was unbuttoned exposing her black bra. They both said they turned slightly to one side and corrected the problem but both said they felt embarrassed. The one with the unzipped skirt had to partially stand up while the other woman had trouble with the buttons. Both said they were concerned that the man might notice and make some silly remark. But their main irritation was with themselves for their carelessness in dressing.

Reducing the signficance of the problem is called for. That can best be done by standing up, excusing oneself, going quickly and directly to a *private* place (holding the skirt closed) and repairing the problem. If this is done quickly, it is quite possible that the man may never have seen the problem. Leaving the scene has the added value that while gone you have time to totally recover from any blushes or signs of embarrassment and can return to your seat as your usual self-confident self.

HAVING TO FACE YOUR PARENT WITH YOUR LOW TEST GRADE

A boy, aged 14, tells of how he was embarrassed when he had to reveal a low test grade to his father. He knew that his father was expecting him to do well and that he would be disappointed. In this case the main approach should be that of making clear that this performance is an accident, is unusual and not part of his usual pattern. If it were, it would not be embarrassing. While he might hope for an understanding father, if such is not the case he must prepare.

He should get up a list of his scores on past exams, lay them out on a piece of paper and *prove* that this performance is a fluke. An alternative is to work out an average score and indicate that this exam only pulls down the score a little. In fact, if enough scores are assembled, the score will have a practically unnoticeable effect.

NOT REALIZING OTHER PERSON HAS
PHYSICAL DISABILITY

This sort of embarrassment is usually felt to be much more serious than it really is. A visitor from Norway, very blond, and dressed in fashionable looking stretch pants and sweater sat down to have a hot chocolate in a ski lodge looking forward to a day on the slopes. A pleasant looking man of about 40 with blue ski cap and pepper and salt beard came by on crutches and sat down across from him. The Norwegian, seeking to be friendly, asked him where he had his accident. The man explained that it was no accident, that he had contracted polio years ago before the Salk vaccine was available. The Norwegian wrote that he felt terribly embarrassed.

> I had opened my mouth, trying to be friendly and look, I really put my foot in it. I didn't know what to say. So after a moment I said "I'm sorry" and got up and left.

Such incidents are rarely as embarrassing to the disabled person as to other person who thinks he has said something awful. Research on the disabled shows they are accustomed to persons not knowing or assuming the wrong thing. What does concern them is that persons will so dread those moments that they will avoid them just as the Norwegian did. This adds a social cost to the real biological cost they already suffer.

At such time then bear in mind that if the other does not seem upset, then you should not be either. If you have such an experience, sit there a moment. You will perhaps discover that the other person is worth talking to, may have an interesting story to tell of how he learned to ski in spite of his disability and does not need or want your sympathy in any way. There is no way you could have known what the other person's trouble was. Your momentary embarrassment will pass quickly and you may have a new friend.

SLIPS OF THE TONGUE AND OTHER
LINGUISTIC NUISANCES

These are the most common of all forms of embarrassment. You mispronounce the name of your closest friend, you stumble or lose your place in a speech, you are guilty of a spoonerism, get your words mixed up or ruin the punch line of a joke by giving away the key word too soon.

Sometimes these bloopers occur in print as in this advertisement which appeared in the *Mexico News,* an Englishlanguage daily in Mexico City:

Doberman. Easy to feed; will eat anything. Especially fond of children. Write (address)

Radio and TV announcers provide many examples since they are on display and audiences are keen to catch even the slightest goof. A sports announcer, speaking of United States victory chances in a recently introduced event at the 1980 Lake Placid Olympics said:

This is a new event for us. So it's probably improbable that we'll win any medals.

Kermit Shafer collected many of these bloopers such as:

(A commercial for a laundry): Ladies who care to drive by and drop off their clothes will receive prompt attention.

144

Since professional announcers are keen to protect their reputations as smooth talkers, they sometimes hurry to correct their errors or pretend they did not occur with even worse results.

> (On a cooking show) So ladies, there is no safer way to insure perfect apple pie each and every time than to use canned sliced apples...So the next time you decide to bake applie pie, go to the can...(PAUSE)...and you will really enjoy sliced piced apples!

The very fact that announcers are expected to be fluent calls our attention to the fact that everyday speakers like us are *not*. We admire the smooth talker but we do not entirely trust him either. The point of everyday spontaneous speech is precisely that it is *not* smooth. Listen to people talking.

> So I...uh...I said to him, Why don't you...why don't you tell me...uh...let's see, what was I saying? Oh yes. . .

That is the very stuff of unrehearsed talk between persons who are at ease with one another. We do not expect fluency and quick to forgive boners or gaffes. If we forgive it in others, we can expect them to forgive it in us when we stumble.

That does not mean they always let it go by. They may smile or laugh. But do not let that upset you. Studies by sociologist Rose Laub Coser show that laughter is a powerful force that binds people together. Think of the last party you were at where you were part of a group that had a good laugh over something. Did it not make you feel good to be part of that group? Or when you hear a cluster of persons on the other side of the room break into laughter, do you not feel somewhat left out?

Persons may still be concerned that when they flub in speaking others are laughing *at* them. Yes, but a slip of the tongue is something that happens to everyone including them. When they smile or laugh they are recognizing themselves in what you have done. The very fact that they continue listening shows they identify with you and are pulling for you to keep going. Do not disappoint them. When you keep moving, it proves you had something to say that was too important to be destroyed by a mere slip of the tongue.

This same way of looking at a slip also applies to those events that are the most important of all. I am referring to the embarrassments that turn up at the great ceremonies of life.

CEREMONIAL FLUBS

We like to think of ourselves as very practical, rational persons. Yet we continue to be thrilled by ceremonies and rituals of all kinds. Apart from religious occasions, we recognize changes of social relationships such as births, namings, birthdays, greetings and farewells, puberty (more so in other societies than ours), graduation, engagement, marriage, decorations, promotions and admissions to office. In addition we may want to confirm relationships as in school daily assemblies where the authority of the principal is reinforced, family gatherings at Thanksgiving to celebrate family solidarity and reunions of all kinds. Further there are physical healing rituals as at Lourdes or confessions and funerals to help restore the bonds of the bereaved to the community. We usually find such occasions fulfilling they can go wrong causing embarrassment.

Flubs are of many kinds. There is the familiar case of the best man who forgets the wedding ring. One person wrote of a christening in which he (the father) on being asked the child's name by the minister totally forgot it until his wife prompted him. Persons may forget their lines at formal ceremonies, the performers can trip on their unaccustomed robes, props can be missing or persons can say totally inappropriate things. One person wrote of a funeral:

> I was a bit late, rushed in to express my condolences to the woman whose husband had died, and then for some reason, after apologizing for being late, I said: "But I'm sure glad to be here." Boy, did I wish I could cut out my tongue!

What can be done about such flubs?

Strange as it may seem, the best man who forgets where he put the ring or any other omission at a ceremonial occasion is less of a problem than in more trivial situations. If he is quite unable to find the ring, the ceremony is too important to be interrupted or embarrassed. The little group around the minister can go right ahead with an imaginary ring (unbeknownst to the audience) and the real ring can be quickly slipped on when the best man does at last find it buried in his coat pocket.

The same goes for funerals, bar mitzvahs, christenings, first communions, confirmations, commemorations and other ritual occasions. Someone may do something wrong but the occasion is felt to be too important to be stopped by any embarrassment. I do not mean to imply that *individuals* will not be embarrassed, sometimes horribly, at their gauche moves, at forgetting lines, at stumbling as they mount the platform. The occasion can still go forth since people will be assumed to be so taken up with its majesty, beauty, or solemnity that the private embarrassments that individuals feel will be felt to be a small price to pay.

One point to remember. If you are the person who committed the flub, do not expect to get off easily. If persons may come up to you and make jokes about your flub accept them bravely. This is one time when you should feel embarrassed, when neither you nor others (nor I) should offer any rescue. You should suffer but silently. Even to make something of your suffering is easily overdone since it can become a little sacrificial ritual of its own and so compete with the big occasion you are there to celebrate. The hope is that people will go away remembering what a grand or solemn occasion it was and not how bad you felt.

PERSONS WHO CANNOT MAKE LIGHT
OF THEIR EMBARRASSMENTS

There remain many persons who simply cannot walk away from embarrassments. These include shy persons about whom we talked in an earlier chapter. They feel so unsure of themselves in company that they even avoid situations which might conceivably cause anything embarrassing to happen. When it does anyhow, they suffer terribly. It is not a minor thing to them. The same is true of persons with low self-esteem. They regard even a minor slip as just confirming the low self-worth they feel.

For both shy persons and those with low self esteem, counseling or psychotherapy may help. But there is one large group of persons who do not require therapy and yet who cannot ever treat their flubs or boo-boos as minor. I am referring to children. Teen agers suffer too but they have enough of the wakening of maturity to realize that they will get over it. Children just cannot look that far ahead.

A mother reported to me that her 7-year old daughter, very proud of the new white party dress she was wearing to a friend's birthday party, was playing on a swing in her friend's backyard with the other guests. She had the misfortune to slip off the swing into a muddy pool of water created by an overnight rain, leaving her dress with gobs of mud on the back.

In spite of the best efforts of her mother and others to remove the mud and their insistence that "nobody cares," the child refused to come out of the bathroom where she was hiding. She insisted that her mother take her home.

For the child, the parent's efforts to dismiss the child's concern as making too much of a minor thing simply shows the parent does not understand. At the child's age, he or she *cannot* make light of it. Children, being very conscious of other people's feelings and judgments but not yet having a self well enough developed to handle such evaluations cannot simply ignore embarrassments. When they say, "I felt awful. I just wanted to die," they mean it.

For the 7-year old whose lovely white dress got muddy, it is important to get her out of the view of others fast. The idea is not to prevent their seeing her for they have. The object instead is to save her as much as possible from the awfulness of what she is sure they are thinking or laughing about.

Sweep her right up and take her to a secluded place where no one is looking. Then ask her whether, after further cleaning up, she feels she can return to the party. If not, get her coat and leave quickly. If early, offer an excuse, race home, change and come back. If late, then leave with whatever explanation seems appropriate.

It is a mistake to tell her she will be "missing all the fun." She is miserable and will not find it fun at all. Above all, do not chide her for being a baby. Her behavior, on the contrary, is not baby-like for babies do *not* get embarrassed. Studies of how children around seven feel about themselves by sociologist Morris

Rosenberg and child psychologist M. D. Lynch show that children have become keenly aware of how they should ideally behave and are concerned for what others think of them. Our seven year old is simply growing up. Adults should not be so quick to feel superior in dismissing children's embarrassments anyhow. I have too many examples of adults who behaved in ways not so different from the 7-year old when they spilled spaghetti sauce on their blouse or dipped their sleeve into the salad dressing. Of course they did not hide in the bathroom but though they tried to dismiss it, or hide it with a napkin, they still felt uncomfortable all evening.

It is not easy to make light of embarrassments. There are times when you can, as we have seen with slips of the tongue, spilling packages and ceremonial flubs. But often, you simply cannot take what has happened lightly. Other strategies are called for.

Chapter 9

Changing Meanings

Things are seldom what they seem
Skim milk masquerades as cream.

So says the chorus in Gilbert and Sullivan's *HMS Pinafore* providing you with a clue on how to handle many embarrassments. You can show that what looks like a failing is really something else, even something admirable.

Changing the meaning as a strategy works differently depending on how important the embarrassing event is. Little embarrassments can be met with a quick reinterpretation such as the word twist in the following case. A junior high school student, hoping to make friends, was looking around the crowded cafeteria while eating a hot-dog. Suddenly the wiener slipped out of the bun. Social psychologist Carolyn Saarni reports what happened next.

> (The wiener) then went skittering across the floor. (The student) felt mortified but managed a laugh and announced... "I guess *that* dog wanted to go for a walk." Everyone laughed and started to joke with him about who would step on the dog's tail first.

Although it took some wit to manage the word shift in meaning, by doing so the student was able to recover by showing himself to be a good sport who could laugh at himself.

Bigger embarrassing events require more than mere word reinterpretations. President Eisenhower found that out when in

1958 he tried to explain away his assistant, Sherman Adams' acceptance of gifts in exchange for what looked like favors. The president tried to tell journalists that "a gift is not necessarily a bribe." It could be simply an expression of friendship. Adams soon resigned.

On the other hand, when Richard Nixon was the running mate in Eisenhower's 1952 presidential campaign, Nixon also faced charges of accepting gifts. He was able however, to convert a gift into something irresistibly positive. In a famous address he admitted only to the gift of a spaniel puppy which his daughter had named Checkers. He went on to say how the children loved the dog and that no matter what anyone said, the family would keep Checkers. The emotional response was overwhelming and Nixon remained on the campaign ticket.

However if the embarrassment is really monumental, you can try anecdoting. This means making the incident into a story worth retelling. Here is what I mean for the cases of small, big and monumental embarrassments.

HANDLING SMALL EMBARRASMENTS

The trick with a small embarrassing incident is to *keep* it small by making a quick reinterpration. Then move on to other things confident that the new meaning you gave the embarrassment disposes of it.

An honest mistake. You pick someone else's raincoat off the rack at a restaurant. Make it into a mock theft by saying with a laugh:

I almost got away with it.

Or you might try:

> All the aptitude tests they gave me showed I didn't have the stuff to make a good thief.

Just rehearsing. At your desk you are thinking intently to the point where you start mumbling in the presence of a fellow worker. Since he or she is now looking at you, you cannot deny mumbling. Try:

> I'm just going over what I'll answer to that SOB Jenkins at the next board meeting if he puts me on the spot again.

If you are asked what you will say, say you are still working on it. Your colleague may even pitch in to help you.

Appealing to a higher motive. A friend finds out you are having a party to which he is not invited. When he confronts you, instead of stumbling, say immediately:

> This is just a payback dinner for all those who've had me over. I didn't mention it to you since I was sure you'd understand and I'd rather not let it get around why I was inviting them and not you.

I assume you will only use such an excuse when that is the real reason. If it is not, then I leave it to your conscience to solve any moral problems. If such an excuse is not for you, then simply saying something like the following will usually do the trick:

> I'll catch you the next time when I have more time to prepare a dinner more to your liking.

There are literally hundreds of situations where we can call upon understandable motives to prevent or explain our way out of embarrassing situations. As parents we often evade sex discussions with our small children because we "don't want them to grow up too fast." We often fool ourselves on that one.

Not wanting to insult or offend someone is an acceptable motive in many situations as when we bravely continue a conversation with a fellow worker in spite of nearly fainting from blasts of his garlic breath. In other situations we use this approach all the time when we refuse a dinner invitation or date or put someone off with an excuse.

That approach has its dangers when we are caught in a lie. But even when we are telling the truth, there can be problems as in a case reported to me of a woman who refused a party invitation because she had to be out of town. As it happened, she was able to get back just hours before the party only to be met at a local supermarket by her would-be host. Although she quite truthfully explained that she had just got back and would be glad to come to the party, the host regretted there just was no more room at the table in his small apartment. Perhaps she might have phoned long distance when she first learned of being able to get home earlier. Then again the relationship may simply not have been a close one to begin with.

Just a stage. A great resource comes from the pop psychology and sociology books at drug store counters and supermarket checkout stands. Such books not only carry authority but provide us with a new vocabulary one of which is the use of "stages" to explain human frailties. Humans are said to be always moving through the "passages" described by author Gail Sheehy or the stages in grieving eloquently traced by Elizabeth Kubler-Ross.

You can draw on these theories to explain away as "normal" what might in an earlier era have been simply embarrassing. When your child is making a nuisance of herself in public and so embarrassing you, you can shake your head while lamenting:

That's what you get from a child in the "terrible twos" (or "exploratory fives")

Similarly husbands who embarrass their wives by preening in front of attractive younger women can be seen as going through a "midlife crisis."

The value of a stage theory is that a stage, by definition, is temporary which the person will pass through. Sometimes it can even be seen as "growth."

DEALING WITH BIGGER EMBARRASSMENTS

Some embarrassments are too important to simply flip away with quick re-interpretations. These include situations where persons are embarrassed by their origins, by prominent blemishes, by being ignored in company, by having someone forget they met you or forgetting names, theirs or yours. All of these hurt too much and call for more complex refashioning of meanings. For these the trick is not to try to make light of them but to make them into something positive that calls for admiration.

EMBARRASSED BY YOUR ROOTS
OR EARLY EXPERIENCES

In the United States for the premiere of one of his movies, Australian actor Mel Gibson brought up an earlier film of his called "Max." He said to an interviewer that he:

> ...was incredibly embarrassed by it. It's not a good film at all. Very 50's, very dated, with this terribly overblown score that drowns the story.

Mr. Gibson's is a common feeling. You may be from a school that others consider degrading or from a small town that others think amusing.

Although you can seek to make light of it by ignoring it or join in the laughter to agree that you consider it of no importance you can try to give it a very different meaning by recognizing that early experiences should be seen to be learning experiences. Mr. Gibson could for example, have pointed out that the film was "a very useful exercise," or one which gave him a chance to learn how it could be done better.

Similarly, a remote school or small town origin can often be handled by reference to something the others do not know about them. Even very obscure schools often have some graduate who went on to fame as did a graduate of Southwest Texas State College named Lyndon B. Johnson. A friend of mine from Prince Albert in Saskatchewan was able to remind me that two Canadian prime ministers were born there.

The most effective strategy of all is take special pride in having humble origins. To have come from Yale or to have had a distinguished teacher is after all, to detract from the enormity of your own achievement.

What this means is that in emphasizing how very humble your origins are, you drive home how far you have come. Mr. Gibson actually did a little of this by adding that he was overwhelmed with all the attention he was getting since even leading actors in Australia are paid much less and treated as quite "ordinary blokes."

The reason I am making much of embarrassment about origins is because some cases that have come to my attention in my research indicate embarrassment about such roots. Still it is possible that such embarrassments are decreasing with the increasing acceptance of diversity in American society. There may even be a reversal with persons now being embarrassed at anything other than poverty-stricken origins. Former President Lyndon B. Johnson when showing reporters around his ranch once claimed that a shack was his early home. The claim was immediately denied by his mother who said he knew very well they had a "nice home" on the farm.

While preparing to do a movie short, Robert Benchley, renowned as a humorous writer and wit, was able to put down his training in classics in a wry observation. The scene called for him to be strung up on telephone wires above a city street. As the props were being prepared, Benchley turned to his wife, Gertrude, saying:

> Remember how good at Latin I was in school?
> Yes.
> Well, look where it got me.

Yet even such self deprecation does not prove that roots no longer count. Quite the contrary. They show more strongly than ever that in the United States humble roots are considered a positive feature of a person's biography. If they have them, persons may point to them as a way of taking credit for how far they have come. If not, persons may either try to point out that they were less blue-blooded than others think or that, as with Benchley, previous distinctions simply count for little.

In politics especially, as suggested above by Lyndon Johnson's attempt to claim a shack as a home, there remains the value of humble origins. When the reverse is true, as was the case with patrician born former President George Bush, the fact is routinely used against them as Ann Richards was able to do in her keynote address to the Democratic party convention in 1992. On national TV, she said:

> Poor George...he can't help it. He was born with a silver foot in his mouth.

The expression was not original with Governor Richards as she herself pointed out. Writer Ralph Keyes, who has carefully researched quotation origins in a book engagingly titled *Nice Guys Finish Seventh*, finds the same expression applied more than 20 years earlier to a New York parks commisioner by a newspaper reporter. All of this simply helps to show that non-humble origins have been a liability for others than George Bush and at previous periods of time.

Pushing humble roots too much has its dangers since it can become a form of inverted pride which may earn you few rewards. It is probably desirable to let lowly origins do their work without much fanfare. Someone such as President Clinton could turn his birthplace of Hope, Arkansas into a motto of his campaign. Others can rest content with referring to something of folk interest about the town or location. You can for example, explain your accent by simply saying that that is how people talk where you come from.

As for myself should it come up, I cannot deny that I was born in Nagy Genez, Roumania. I remember nothing about it since my parents brought me as a babe in arms to Canada where I grew up. I have however researched it. Nagy Genez turns out to be in Transylvania, Dracula country. I may have some eminent ancestors after all but I do not think I can take any pride in them.

BLEMISHES

In spite of the insistence of psychotherapists that we should be "honest" and "authentic," we do not escape the fact that personal blemishes are often felt to be embarrassing. Some of these, to use the everyday and not always pleasant way persons refer to them, include warts, birthmarks, prominent scars, pimples, cauliflower ears, cross-eyes, potbellies, very large or very small breasts, bunions, bow-legs, knock-knees, buck teeth, baldness, excess hair, a receding chin and much more.

It does not really help obese women to be told by anthropologists that Greek men are turned on by such women or that in some Melanesian societies a fat wife is considered to symbolize her husband's affluence. The problem is that Western middle class society, which tends to dominate conceptions of taste, continues to celebrate the classic photographers' fashion model who is *not* fat.

We may be able to change standards but we cannot get rid of invidious comparisons altogether. For the sad fact as attested to by anthropology itself as well as all the social sciences is that although societies vary in what they regard as beautiful, no society exists or ever has existed which has no standards of beauty. Then what can can we do about our blemishes?

We can change their meaning but this time make them into something positive. One of my ears is pointed almost as much as that of Mr. Spock of *Star Trek* fame. What I have done with that blemish is make it into an item of identification. Since I have no visible scars or other marks, I have something to fill in on legal forms that is unique: Pointed left ear. I have found that immigration and other officials are quite interested and ask to see it.

I am not claiming that every blemish can be given an alternate meaning. But if you cannot hide yours and it bothers you, then I suggest you seek a positive way of dealing with the nervous attempts others make not to look at it or avoid mentioning it for fear of upsetting you. Few of us can go as far as actors Jimmy Durante or Danny Thomas who made their large noses into marks of identity and central parts of comedy routines. Still we can try for other reinterpretations.

If you are bald or nearly so and it bothers you, you can hint that the evidence is that baldness goes with sexual potency. If you are blessed with unusually large or so-called "cauliflower" ears, it is not helpful to hide or ignore the fact that others are being careful to look you straight in the eye. You can call attention to them. When someone starts to repeat what they said, thinking you did not hear them, you can assure the speaker that "with these ears, I pick up more than people realize."

Obese persons in the United States have a special problem with the "keeping fit" pressures that are so much celebrated among the young. There seems now to be a counter pressure operating, even a movement among overweight women to re-define standards of beauty. Some TV personalities are obese without apparent concern though some of them are seen to go on diets from time to time. Perhaps there may be changes coming to weight standards but doctors do continue to warn of health dangers.

Each of us will have to decide what is best. BUT if you give up on diets and decide to accept your weight for what it is, then a positive interpretation is worth trying for. Being fat and glad of it enables you to say "yes!" with zest when your host offers you a second piece of pie while you add:

> Since you have gone to the trouble of serving such a glorious pie, it's a sin not to finish it.

Most persons try to avoid bringing up the subject of weight for fear of offending you. If it comes up, often in indirect form in talks about diets or low calorie desserts, listen tolerantly to the tales of (usually temporary) triumphs over weight and then say:

> I just don't have time or patience for all that. I am what I am and I don't try to change it. I love food and I'm not giving it up until my doctor tells me to. I also make sure I see only doctors who are fatter than I am.

They are likely to laugh with you and change the subject.

BEING IGNORED IN A GROUP

You are having coffee with two persons when they suddenly move onto some topic that you know nothing about nor can be expected to know anything about. They talk of the fun they had at a party they attended or get into a discussion of details of some common interest (such as high real estate prices, problems of their teen-age children or how hard it is to get a good gardener these days) which interest you do not share.

The temptation is to put up tolerantly with such talk and wait for them to get through so you can get back in. I strongly suggest you *do not do that* . What they have done is a hostile act. It is unintentional but still they have excluded you from the group and you should not let an offense to your self as a worthy person go unchallenged. What can you do?

I suggest that you do not sit there with an embarrassed look on your face or try to participate, however inadequately with a "How interesting," or "I didn't know that." If such a discussion continues for as long as a full minute, take action. Have a last sip of coffee, interrupt and say, "You two have a lot to talk about so I'll be on my way." Then get up and leave.

When you do that, you are *redefining the situation* from a shared conversation of three persons to a private conversation of just the other two. Your departure is quite appropriate. The ball is now in their court if they wish to re-define it back to a group of three again.

They will probably try, with apologies to you, and then you can decide whether you want to accept their re-definition or not. If not you can insist that you have to leave. Whether you go this far is up to you, how much you value their friendship or how serious the exclusion was. If it was a minor thoughtless exclusion, then simple apologies should be enough to get you to change your mind. If they were really treating you badly (say talking about the high price of domestic help when you are having trouble paying your rent) then perhaps you do not need their friendship or it never really existed anyhow.

SOMEONE YOU MET RECENTLY DOES NOT REMEMBER YOU

You know this problem if you are (or ever were) a high school or college aged boy who has met a girl at a large gathering such as a "get acquainted" party. Alas, one thing that does *not* happen at such occasions is any getting acquainted. There are just too many persons, introductions are brief and persons circulate so they can hardly get to know anything about each other. But let us say you, a boy at such an occasion, met an attractive girl whom you would like to get to know better. After several fearful approaches to the telephone, you get up your courage and phone her. When she answers, you say:

> Hi! This is Tommie Murdoch.
> She says, "Who?"

The conversation has now reached a dismal point, and your inclination is to get it over with as quickly as possible and hang up. You think, 'What made me imagine she'd remember a loser like me?' What should you do to overcome your embarrassment at such a reception?

Counselors who have researched this problem coach their clients not to retaliate as embarrassed people often do. For instance the urge of many college age persons is to act hurt (as they are), and say:

> Don't you remember me?

Or many boys will make attempt at humor by saying:

Don't tell me you don't remember the handsome guy with the winning smile!

It is no surprise that these attempts fail since it is you, after all, who has really put the girl on the spot in the first place. It is up to you to make it easy for her to respond. You should answer in a straightforward manner with more information. After she says, "Who?", you might say:

Tom Murdoch. We met at the garden party a couple of days ago. I was wearing a green tweed sport coat, and we talked about the fact that we were both from Sacramento.

What you are doing is *re-interpreting* the forgetting of your name. Most of us are very poor at name remembering especially at such a time. So her failure to remember your name doesn't mean she might not remember you. With a little help, she probably will or will appreciate your efforts enough to at least want to see you again. It's worth a try. This method works for older persons too.

FORGETTING NAMES OR GETTING THEM WRONG

This brings us to a very common source of embarrassment. Let me give you an example from my own experience. I met a man named Holmes whom I wanted to and expected to meet again. I wanted to remember his name. I have read books on this subject. I even took a course on it once. The major advice I got was to try to associate something distinctive (and unusual) about the person's appearance that will tie him to his name. I stared at

Holmes, searching for some clue, when I noticed that he had unusually large, rather floppy ears. Presto! Big floppy ears suggested a hunting dog, and from that I free-associated to Sherlock *Holmes* who was fond of wearing a hunting cap, with ear flaps. I snapped my fingers in self-congratulation for that clever connection.

A couple of weeks later, I ran into him again at a luncheon, marched right up to him confidently, stuck out my hand, and said:

> "Ah, there you are, Mr. Otis. I still remember that interesting talk we had a couple of weeks ago."

Mr. Holmes looked at me like I had gone bonkers. When he told me his actual name, was *I* embarrassed. You see, Otis is the name of my daughter's dog. Association alone can lead just as easily to the wrong associations.

What then should you do? There are three steps. The first two are standard in memory training. The third suggests you follow our approach in this chapter by changing the meaning of the encounter.

Step 1: Listen for the name. You only remember what you hear.

Step 2: Do try for some association, the more ridiculous the better.

Step 3: TRANSFORM THE FIRST MEETING INTO AN OCCASION FOR REMEMBERING THE PERSON'S NAME

How do you do that? Exaggerate the importance of the name. Dwell on it. Ask him to spell it. If at all odd, visibly write it down and repeat it several times. If he hesitates or seems embarrassed at this attention, tell him you *want* to remember the name and that you are terrible at remembering names. Tell him that since you can only remember a limited number, you have to concentrate on the really important ones.

You may think I am overdoing this. In his best seller on winning friends, Dale Carnegie wrote:

> Remember that a man's name is to him the sweetest and most important sound in any language.

If alive today, I am sure he would say that applies to women as well. Although Dale Carnegie is often maligned as simply endorsing manipulative strategies, he offers persuasive support on how important names are to their bearers. Being able to recall someone's name seems an essential skill whatever your goals may be. If you follow the three steps suggested above, you *will* remember the person's name and you can earn a bonus. If you take the trouble to occasionally repeat your own name as you emphasize his, that person will remember yours too.

FOR THE REALLY MONUMENTAL EMBARRASSMENTS: TRY ANECDOTING

Exaggeration in remembering names provides a clue on how to manage the truly awful embarrassments that you feel the worst about. Do you remember the sad story of the hapless diplomat who caught his tie in his fly? Back on page 32, I told of how the embarrassment that followed ruined his career. He had become such a laughing stock that his usefulness as a dignified diplomat was destroyed. That is what I mean by a monumental embarrassment. Is there anything he could have done to save the situation?

We get a hint by looking at another monumental embarrassment, one that has become famous. On one occasion, a well known radio announcer named Harry Von Zell had the honor of introducing the 31st president of the United States. Since it is always assumed that the president needs no "words of introduction," Mr. Von Zell simply said:

> Ladies and gentlemen, the President of the United States, Hoobert Heever!

The incident has become famous as an illustration that even professional polished announcers can garble an introduction.

I must now ask. Do you know what Mr. Hoover spoke about at that time? No matter how good an historian you are, I feel sure you do not. Why? Because Mr. Von Zell's blooper has become possibly more memorable than anything Mr. Hoover might have said.

That is our clue. When you experience a really monstrous embarrassment, do not try to hide it or make light of it. Instead, TRANSFORM IT INTO AN ANECDOTE. Embellish it by adding little details so that it becomes a rollicking story that people enjoy hearing.

I do not know if Mr. Hoover did more than merely smile at the blooper or if Mr. Von Zell did more than just blush and hope everyone would forget it . Of course they never have. He should have recognized that he was present at what was surely an historic occasion, however minor. He might then have said:

167

Mr. President. May I say two things? First, I apologize. Second, you have been called many names by Democrats and Republicans alike. But I'll bet this is the first time in your political career that anyone has ever called you Mr. Heever!

If Mr. Von Zell had said those words I imagine the president would have roared with laughter and the radio audience would have enjoyed it as well. It would be their main topic of conversation later.

As for our hapless diplomat who caught his tie in his zipper, he too might have tried to make his experience into an anecdote. Perhaps at the next public occasion when called upon to say something he might have said:

Some of you may be surprised to see me tonight. Many of you perhaps thought that I had gone into the tie business, bow ties of course. I must say it has occurred to me. I cannot choose between that and possibly the pants business, pants with buttons.

I do not know whether he would have been capable of that sort of recovery or whether his usefulness as a diplomat had already been totally destroyed. But it is one way of rescuing his reputation since people are not likely to forget the embarrassing incident . Instead of hiding it, he can show himself to be a good sport, a person who can handle himself and in the end a likable person who might turn out to be an excellent diplomat after all.

Chapter 10

Managing Your Identities

The key to embarrassment is what happens to your identity. You have staked out a claim that you are a certain kind of person with certain skills or abilities. Then suddenly something happens that throws doubt on those claims. You are revealed as not being the person others assumed you were. Your identity is inappropriate or has become discredited.

If you cannot deny the significance of your failure or cannot change its meaning, then you can try to *manage your identity*. You can try to show that the person who did the embarrassing thing was not the real you. I begin with some simple ways of doing so.

NOT YOURSELF

One of the simplest ways of handling identity is to insist that you were not your usual self because you were sick or sleepy from having been up half the night with a collicky baby. You can often be forgiven or excused if you have something weighty on your mind. A bankrupt businessman who is desperately trying to pay off his creditors hardly needs to explain why he failed to show up at a cocktail party. Others are understandably so overcome with grief or sadness at the loss of a friend or relative that their failure to acknowledge greetings is not felt to be an embarrassment at all.

Having something heavy on your mind is not necessarily something you have to trouble to explain. It is often simply assumed by others as a way to account for what would otherwise be seen as a slight or thoughtlessness. One of my repondents told of a married neighbor couple who had to leave their Golden Retriever home while they were away at work. They would try to return once or twice during the day since if gone for long periods, the dog would howl ceaselessly. They would then have to apologize explaining that extra work had prevented their coming home. However on the news that they were getting a divorce, all the neighbors immediately seized on that as the obvious reason for any neglect of the dog. Instead of anger, howling would be met with offers to take care of the dog whenever either might want assistance.

SHIFTING RESPONSIBILITY FROM YOURSELF

You can escape embarrassment if you can show that your identity is not discredited since you were not responsible in the first place. The simplest cases are those where we blame our poor performance on poor lighting or excuse our perspiration by calling attention to stuffiness or hot lights. The excuse did not work for violinist Mischa Elman. He and virtuoso pianist Leopold Godowsky were in the audience at a performance by the child prodigy Jascha Heifetz who was playing brilliantly. During a break, Elman took out his handkerchief to mop his brow remarking to Godowsky:

It's awfully hot in here

Godowsky looked at him and then said slyly:

Not for pianists.

A common and abused excuse is to blame having to ask embarrassing questions on some bureaucratic requirement. For example an insurance adjuster may ask a battery of questions about your personal life. To excuse such prying into personal affairs, the questions may be prefaced by something like: "I hate to ask these personal questions but it's company policy."

Such an explanation may save the adjuster from embarrassment but it may leave us embarrassed or at least irritated. Sometimes you can if really upset, challenge the claim and occasionally you will find that there is really no good reason for asking the questions or making some other bureaucratic demand.

This is what Alan M. Dershowitz succeeded in doing when he was a young assistant professor of law at Harvard. Since he was an observant Jew, he was upset when he found he had to teach classes on Saturday, the Jewish Sabbath. When he asked for a different schedule, Dean Erwin Griswold said he could not shift his assignment without being unfair to others. But why, Dershowitz asked, are classes held on Saturday? The dean replied that it was simply a practice that had grown up over the years. Later, after presumably concluding there was no need for the practice, the dean changed it.

I am not arguing that we can all act as boldly as Mr. Dershowitz. Still occasionally an objection or a call to a bureaucrat's supervisor can produce change. You are showing that personal questions or other objectionable procedures are offensive to your identity and are probably not even necessary.

Sometimes responsibility can be escaped when persons can legitimately claim they lacked knowledge. A respondent who had not seen a woman acquaintance for a long period asked her innocently what her husband was "doing these days." He was met with this sour response:

What is he doing? Two years, for fraud.

He asked me what he might have done about the embarrassment. I first reminded him of suggestions in one of our previous chapters on the need to prepare carefully. Whenever you have not seen someone for a long time, it is wise not to assume you can take up where you left off. Not only prison but divorce, death, job loss and many other changes are not only possible but likely to have occurred. The British statesman Disraeli is credited with greeting old acquaintances with the all-purpose line:

And how is the old complaint?

To which anthologist Clifton Fadiman adds a quotation for an all-purpose line for intellectuals or literary persons:

How's the book?

The suggestion then, is to proceed cautiously with general questions allowing the others to bring anything up if they choose.

For the man who was confronted with information on the woman's husband's prison term, it is of course too late for prevention. I suggested he should simply reply, quite innocently, "I didn't know," then wait to see if she wants to talk about if. If not, shift to another subject. Although he did open up the subject of the woman's husband, he can hardly be held responsible for what happened next. One could even argue that the revelation was so startling and unexpected, that he was put on the spot. A quick withdrawal is needed.

POINTING TO ANOTHER IDENTITY

For some potentially embarrassing situations persons can claim their identity is temporary or taken on for a special purpose. The present identity may call for a costume or kind of behavior which will be cast aside after one's duties are completed.

For example, actor Ted Danson who for years played the part of Sam Malone, the bartender and lead in the long-running TV series CHEERS, wore a hairpiece on the show. Offstage and particularly when he worked in the environmentalist movement, he removed it letting his thinning hair show. He (or his director) felt a hairpiece was appropriate for what was a strongly romantic role.

Danson himself explained:

When I play Sam Malone, I wear a hairpiece. When I'm an environmentalist, I don't. Somehow it sets me straight.

Although it involved shyness rather than embarrassment, a case cited by psychologist Philip G. Zimbardo involves a similar identity shift. A young woman he calls Laura was so shy she could hardly state her name in class without blushing. Yet she worked part time as a nude model for male photographers for $20 an hour. She said that though she would hardly be able to appear nude in front of friends while, for example, skinny dipping, she had no difficulty in the role of model even before men who only pretended to take pictures so they could ogle her. She said:

> After I started modelling I very quickly began to see the people who came as objects just as they saw me. Then it became very easy.

Others in embarrassing roles may similarly be able to distance themselves from those roles by showing a more admirable side which should not be forgotten. Sociologist Laud Humphreys has written of the cover of what he calls "refulgent respectability" which persons in deviant activities often employ. A study of workers in a motel that was a sexual rendezvous for prostitutes and others revealed that the workers were at considerable pains to point out that this work was "just a job" and that they led highly conventional lives outside. The talk of those workers was peppered with what happened at the church social last night, a forthcoming marriage of one of their children or a sharing of opinions of the standard TV shows which they, like millions of middle Americans, enjoyed watching.

A related device is showing the "me" that was guilty of some embarrassing performance cannot be the real me because the speaker comes from a group which is way above such things. An experiment by psychologists R. B. Cialdini and K. D. Richardson asked students to evaluate their own university, Arizona State University in comparison with cross-state rival the University of Arizona. Beforehand students had taken what was called a "creativity test" after which some were told they had done poorly and the rest received no feedback.

The students who were told they had done poorly and thus suffered some loss of self-esteem and probably embarrassment showed a stronger tendency to exaggerate the qualities of their own university over that of the other. The results are interpreted as an attempt to restore their self-esteem by pointing to their membership in an obviously superior institution. It was as if they were saying: "Maybe I'm not creative but that's not important compared to the fact that I'm a student at a very superior university. "

Persons whose work is of low status or personally embarrassing such as bailbondsmen, garbage collectors, and city street workers frequently adopt a similar strategy. They will be careful to point out their works is not as stigmatizing as others might think. Sociologist David S. Davis reports from his research on bailbondsmen that they are often seen as "parasites who feed off the misfortunes of others." In their own defense, they argue that in addition to performing the essential service of keeping people out of jail, their work requires, in the words of one:

> ...the knowledge of attorneys, police officers, investigators, collection agencies, car salesmen, court clerks, judges and loan officers and bankers.

Clearly there is nothing embarrassing about company like that.

Similarly those doing heavy physical work will make it clear that no one else has the stamina to put up with the demands of their work. Studies of apartment house janitors by sociologist Raymond L. Gold reveal that though their tenants look down on them, the janitors gain a sense of superiority from what the garbage itself reveals. Although the janitors do not relish the job, the fact that they must sort the garbage brings to view many unopened bills as well as other revelations of shameful acts .Such knowledge helps erase, at least from their own minds, any sense of embarrassment about their occupation. The views of others are dismissed as those of ignorant persons.

Next let us turn to complex embarrassments that have been reported to me in my own research.

WHAT TO DO WHILE THEY SING "HAPPY BIRTHDAY"

Unless you have advanced to a remarkable age which few make, it is difficult to feel pride at your birthday party. Since it is scarcely an achievement, you are left feeling inadequate. You are being honored for something for which you really cannot take much credit. Yet there they are happily shouting, in and out of tune, "Happy birthday, dear Horace, happy birthday to you–oo–oo!" How should you handle your embarrassment at all this attention?

What you can do is to change your conception of your identity. Instead of thinking of yourself as "the one being honored today," change it to "I am providing an occasion for them to enjoy themselves."

They really are. Think back to the birthday parties you attended as a child or even at other times. Did you not look forward to them? Not just for the food or the games and prizes but because of the special mood that pervades birthday parties. People are on their best behavior as usual animosities are suppressed in the interests of honoring the birthday boy or girl (of whatever age). No one wants to spoil it for them. Even envy of presents is suppressed as the honored one opens each one expressing proper appreciation for every gift however small.

I am not saying that such parties are always successful or that people really do have a good time. Envy of or even dissastifaction with presents is only suppressed and animosities

176

are merely kept under control. Nor do people suddenly become friends. Still as the birthday honoree, you are providing a welcome pause in the ongoing rush, a bit of peace in the war of social relations as well as a delicious birthday cake.

Therefore recognize all the fine things that are happening because you are having a birthday. Do not sit with eyes downcast. Look around at each person singing and smile as you see the gladness in their eyes. They are enjoying themselves and grateful that you invited them. They are amused to see their friends all dressed up in party clothes and most of all delighted to see you in your grand role as host and author of all this merriment.

BEING TOO GOOD LOOKING

This may seem like a strange source of embarrassment but several persons have reported such problems to me. They are not boasting. It is something like the problem of the birthday person who is experiencing a lot of attention but it has its own features.

Sometimes these persons are commercial models and some are actors. Their good looks lead to their being stared at by strangers with the result that some complain of embarrassment.

Some part of the embarrassment occurs because the excess attention they receive interferes with their desire to act and relate to people in a natural spontaneous way. The feeling that others are paying attention to their looks rather than to what they are saying, is faintly unnerving and irritating. For once these men share in the complaint of many women who are seen as females first rather than as the whole persons they are. While such a focus is taking place, persons feel as if they are on a stage or as if they are freaks who must perform for the benefit of the staring crowd.

Some of these men have reported to me that they also suffer from a fear that they are suspected of having too high an opinion of themselves. Others feel they can take no credit for their good looks (perhaps their parents should receive the "credit") and are therefore receiving attention that is not really deserved.

If you are such a person, let me offer some suggestions. The main way to handle this embarrassment is to change your identity, that is, the way you think about yourself. You *are* doing something for which you *do* deserve credit. You are providing people with the opportunity to take pleasure in the admiration of an object of beauty. People pay admission charges to go to an art gallery to view the beautiful paintings and sculpture pieces. Handsome men and attractive women make more believable heroes and heroines in pictured love stories on TV or in the movies.

So you must accept the gift that your parents have provided you with not simply as something to be hidden away or as even something you are a bit ashamed of. Instead, you are *the steward of an art object* whose display gives pleasure.

Further, it *is* an accomplishment to display that object to maximum advantage to those that would see. It would be easy for you to hide your attractive face and/or figure with ill-fitting clothes, unkempt hair, ill-trimmed beard, lack of sleep and other kinds of neglect. Just as a museum curator will be careful to dust his paintings (if glass enclosed), and make sure the light in the room shows them off to maximum effect, so too you have a duty to take care that others will enjoy you to maximum effect.

This does *not* mean showing off or strutting along the beach as if you were at a fashion show. It means taking basic care that you look neat and clean, dress normally and move as easily as people will let you in company. When people stare, smile back and should any actually compliment you, accept with a gracious thanks and move on in your conversation to the next subject.

CAUGHT AT HOME

You are at home when normally you would be at work. You are working at home, have taken some deserved time off or are not feeling well. A neighbor or friend rings the doorbell and you answer. You are in a state of partial undress, perhaps unshaven, hair unkempt and wearing a seedy old T-shirt or soiled slacks.

Persons who have described situations like this say they feel the need to make an apology, explain why they are at home or why they are not dressed to receive company. Often they make a limp response, even lie and feel uneasy about the whole thing.

The basic response is to frame your conduct in terms of identity. Most of us when caught in this sort of scene sense that we are acting inappropriately to our identity. We fall back into the role we would assume if we were at the office or shop.

We are not at the office. Our dress and appearance is actually *entirely appropriate* for the identity we have: someone at home who does not have to be prepared for visitors.

In such a situation, if you feel the need you can offer a brief account:

Hi. I'm doing some things at home today where I need privacy.

Or for a minor illness:

Hi. I'm a bit out of it today. So I'll check with you tomorrow.

Often that will be a clear enough signal to anyone you know who might want to spend time with you (unless of course you do want to see that person). The point is to accept what you are and your appropriate dress and not feel any guilt.

STREET EMBARRASSMENTS ADDRESSED TO PASSING WOMEN

This is one of the common forms of public harassment experienced by women, especially the employed, when they walk down busy city streets. Sociologist Carol Brooks Gardner carried on careful observational studies in a large American city in which she reports seeing: a woman being followed down the street by a truck whose driver had the air brakes emit a noise every few feet, two members of a crew of workers belching heartily as a woman passed, men jingling their change in their pockets loudly as they walked past women and a man tapping his magazine as a woman passed him.

To explain such conduct, Brooks believes that women in urban areas are being treated as "open persons." An open person is anyone who can be approached or talked to at will as, for example, a person walking a pedigreed dog or a man with a complex camera kit. Strangers often feel they are free to ask about the dog or camera without being seen as invading the others' privacy. Women, Brooks feels, are treated in this way also especially if young and moderately attractive.

Why women are so treated is not clear from research. My own hypothesis is that there is an element of aggressiveness in such remarks in that the women are treated as if their right to be out in the open at all is being questioned.

European social scientists Cheryl Benard and Edit Schlaffer interviewed 60 men who made uninvited remarks to them on the streets of Vienna. Most expressed surprise that women found their remarks offensive. The social scientists hazard the explanation that for working class men who make such remarks to middle class women, the behavior is a kind of a class revolt. On the other hand, when tradition-bound middle class men make such remarks, they may be expressing resentment at the invasion by women of the masculine world.

Although the men may feel the remarks are not offensive, most women find them not only embarrassing but are incensed by them, even seeing them as analagous to rape. Often they are full of obvious double-entendre.

In the United States research, sociologist Gardner reports the following events. A woman passing by with a cat carrier with two cats in it heard passing males say loudly that is a "mighty fine pussy there." A man passing a woman with prominent breasts remarked to a companion that cantaloupes are cheap this time of year.

When the remark seems innocent, the woman may respond with polite thanks not realizing that such a response, however innocent may be taken as an invitation for sexual engagement. Gardner reports:

> A middle-aged man in Santa Fe pleasantly tells a young-middle-aged woman how lovely her dress is.
> When she thanks him, he offers to take the dress off for her.

What can be done about such engagements? There is a considerable advice literature in popular magazines which offers various tactics and many women act on that advice. Some suggestions include: dressing unattractively, avoiding a "provocative" walk and trying to by-pass the threat by taking a different route. Although helpful, such tactics place on women the tiresome task of always having to be on guard as well as the sheer extra time wasted by such preparations.

Some of the literature suggests outright hostility as in a comment of Journalist Lindsay Van Gelder who writes of a response to a remark:

How'dja like to be in my stable, baby?

Yeah. Who are you—the horse's ass?

Since women are usually infuriated by the remarks, such a response seems no more than deserved. The danger is that such a response or any response can easily lead to an escalation. The man will respond with an even more insulting and not subtle remark. The result can be that unless she is prepared to continue, she may find the whole thing disgusting and impossible to handle. There may even be violence as men feel they must prove their masculinity or rescue what they feel is their wounded pride.

More practical and safer tactics are proposals to simulate an escort. These cater to the stereotype of the helpless female and are well known to most women. The tactics include asking a friend to accompany one at night as well as formalized devices such as the "ride switchboards" found on college campuses. Some women are reported as placing items such as a man's hat or pipe on the car seat, although some report being rather embarrassed at resorting to such pretexts.

An adaptation of the escort approach it to try effecting a transformation of identity. For example, if you are confronted by a group of male department store clerks who appear to be making wise cracks to one another, you might try approaching one directly and asking for assistance in making a purchase. The whole tone changes and the man is likely to act out his role with ease. What you are doing is calling on him to act the part of sales assistant which, after all, is what he is.

Sociologist Gardner mentions the case of a woman who on approaching a construction site, nodded in a friendly manner and greeted the men before they had a chance to make any remarks. These devices turned the tables as the woman came on not as a depersonalized female but a whole friendly person.

Another way of transforming your identity is to adopt a variation on what Lindsay van Gelder calls the "rent a man" ploy. As you prepare to walk down the street and see you are approaching a danger spot such as a construction site where men are sitting around eating lunch, look around for a couple or if possible a family and fall into step with them. You are changing your identity from lone passer-by to member of a respected group.

We are left wondering how long women will have to go through with such masquerades. For now the street behavior seems to be entrenched in males. Perhaps the next generation of men, accustomed to women in all workplaces and other settings, will feel less threatened and be able to turn to more challenging and more dignified pursuits.

Chapter 11

Social Moves

We have been considering how you handle an embarrassment by reducing its significance, changing its meaning or managing your identity. All those strategies are things you do yourself. Now I want to show you some techniques which involve bringing in other persons.

ALTERCASTING

Apart from managing your own identity, you can often do something about the other person's identity. This tactic is what sociologists Eugene Weinstein and Paul Deutschberger call "altercasting." You impose an identity on someone else ("alter") and hope that person will accept it.

When, for example, embarrassed by your child's whining for some favorite food in the supermarket, you can say to the child:

> Hey, you don't want these people to think you're a baby, do you?

Or for an older child you can cast him into the role of a supporter of your reputation as provider:

> Do you want all these people to think I don't give you enough to eat at home?

185

When short of money you can turn to a companion and altercast:

> As a friend I hope I can count on you to take care of the bill. (Pause) Please?

Sometime, when about to tell a spicy story, you may try to fend off embarrassment by warning:

> If any of you are embarrassed by sex, you better use ear plugs because this one will make you blush so much people will think you're sunburned."

Since few like to admit they can be easily embarrassed, you have in effect gotten a sort of permission to go ahead. Still your story had better be good or you will be the one embarrassed.

SHIFTING STANDARDS

Since embarrassment often involves a failure to measure up to some group's ideal standard of behavior, one thing you can do is to insist that standard may apply to others but not to you. For a particularly garbled twist of language you can say:

> As you might gather, I've given up my plans to audition for anchorperson for the evening news.

If caught sinning, instead of embarrassed denials or explanation you can (if the sin is not too serious) shrug your shoulders as you say:

> Well I never claimed to any sort of goody-two-shoes.

A variant of this tactic is to identify with some group that has standards that are more appropriate to your behavior. You may be below par with one group but point out that you belong to another group where doing whatever you did is not considered embarrassing. Almost any failure can be dismissed with the classic line: "I guess I must be getting old." Or:

> The Shady Rest Old Folks Home turned down my application. After I tell them about this I'll bet they give me a special rate.

Related sorts of escapes for younger persons include concessions that they are not in line for the debate team in school or for the precision marching band.

I suggest using this tactic only with minor embarrassments. If your goof is really serious, there is danger the other will simply agree with you.

REPAIRING DAMAGE

Embarrassment often does damage. By "damage" I mean that it interrupts something important or discredits an identity which somebody values highly. Michael Holroyd, a British biographer, tells of being at a small dinner in which the guest of honor was a member of the royal family. She was an excellent mimic, first doing a regional British accent and then a perfect Irish one. Holroyd was carried away and when she spoke again, bellowed with laughter adding:

> Do it again, Ma'am. That one's *priceless*.

Suddenly he noticed that there was dead silence as everyone stared at him. She had been talking in her own voice. Clearly some damage had been done to the easy flow of relationships at the party, not to speak of Mr. Holroyd's chances of being invited to future exclusive parties.

A clue on what to do at such times is provided by results of laboratory experiments in which persons are deliberately asked to do some embarrassing thing. In every case persons try to save face.

Psychologists Bert R. Brown and Howard Garland had subjects sing "Love is a Many Splendored Thing" in front of persons said to be experts. Some of the singers were told the experts rated them well and others that they were rated poorly. Then they were asked to sing before another audience and this time they were paid for singing according to how long they sang. Those who had been told they sang poorly cut short their singing even though it cost them money to do so.

Other experiments showed that embarrassed persons were glad to help out in a very boring task to help restore their self-esteem. Still other studies show persons full of excuses and justifications. Although persons try to hide their embarrassment, British social psychologists Robert J. Edelmann and Sarah E. Hampson videotaped reactions which showed embarrassed persons could not conceal telltale signs of nervous hand and leg movements as well as tendencies to lower their eyes.

When persons are embarrassed by damage they have done, they do all of the above as well as wanting desperately to try to repair the damage. It is almost as if they want to do penance to restore other persons' favorable view of them.

If damage can be repaired, as when you break something or hurt someone, then concrete compensation can be offered. But what about the case of Mr. Holroyd? When no obvious compensation is possible, we are left with just one alternative: apologize. I suspect that is what Mr. Holroyd did.

An apology is no simple thing. Although it sounds easy, if sincere it suggests something quite complex as sociologist Erving Goffman sees it. When you offer an apology, you split your self into two parts: the part that did the deed and the part that rejects the part that did the deed. The apology itself has these elements:

    a. an expression of the embarrassment itself
    b. making it clear you know how you should have behaved
    c. expressing agreement with any punishment as deserved
    d. verbal reprimand of oneself
    e. avowal of intent never to repeat the performance.
    f. performance of penance
    g. volunteering of compensation if possible

That ought to be enough! Notice that you are not only covering yourself with abasement. You are also subtly letting the other know that you are not so far down the road as not to be admitted back into the community. Your apology itself you hope, does the job of showing you are worthy of forgiveness and absolution on the spot. One result, as we know from our own experience, is that if the apology is seen as sincere, the one you have offended is often quick to say: "Oh, that's quite alright. I understand." Apologies often do work.

Let me now turn to a complex but very common case of embarrassment reported to me and how we might handle it using some of the conclusions from the research I have mentioned. Then we will turn to other cases.

A GUEST AT YOUR DINNER PARTY
KNOCKS OVER HIS WINE GLASS

You are the beaming host or hostess proud of what has up to now been a highly successful dinner. The hors d'oeuvres have been universally admired, the gaspacho soup perfect and the beef stroganoff has made your guests smack their lips in satisfaction. Everyone is now sitting around the table sipping their coffee.

In front of one of your guests is a half consumed glass of wine. As he turns to reach for a sprig of grapes from the fruitplate, his elbow hits his wine glass cleanly and over it goes. Sploosh. Let me assume finally, that you have a white linen tablecloth and the wine is a red Burgundy.

The irresistible urge of hosts and hostesses I have seen is to make light of it presumably to make the guest feel he has done no serious harm. Meanwhile all the evidence is that harm *has* been done. The host or hostess will have dashed out only to return with two large bath towels to stuff under the tablecloth to protect the polished mahogany surface of the table. In one incident that I witnessed, the hostess, while busily mopping up and inserting towels, kept reassuring the unhappy guest that it was "O.K." and insisting that his apologies were quite unneeded. We spent the next hour continuing our talk with the mound of towels sitting there precariously in front of the erring guest.

When such a thing happens to you as host or hostess, let me suggest you do something different. Try drawing a lesson from the laboratory research I have outlined. That research showed that when people are embarrassed, they feel like clods. Their self-esteem has been wounded and they want to *do something* to restore it. They will do almost anything not simply to repair the damage but to make up somehow for their wounded face.

As host or hostess *provide your guest with an opportunity to do so*. This means not making light of it. Your guest can see you are trying to make him feel better and that just makes it worse. It is obvious something serious has happened and you take him for a fool if you try to claim nothing has.

Whether any damage has been done to your tablecloth (or table) or not, damage *has* been done to the man's identity. His image of himself as an esteemed guest in total command of his body has now been spoiled. He *must* act. His hands are moving nervously and so are his legs.

I suggest you give him the chance to participate in the cleanup. Give him a couple of towels. Ask him to please move the tablecloth back. If it needs soaking in cold water, which is likely, have him help clear the table so as to remove everything.

After he has had a chance to participate to a maximum extent in helping and removing things, move everyone away from the scene. Suggest that everyone now move into the living room "where we can all be more comfortable." No one, especially the guest, needs to continue staring at the mess. The guest having done some penance for his sin and everyone chatting easily in the living room, you can now graciously offer forgiveness by saying to him:

> Now then, you didn't finish your wine. Let me get you another.

He will probably refuse with something like:

> Me? I'm a teetotaler from here on—at least for the rest of this evening!

Everyone will likely enjoy a laugh. He will still feel something of a klutz but less so than if you had tried to make light of the whole thing.

YOUR PET MESSES YOUR NEIGHBOR'S LAWN

This one seems a long way from incidents we have considered such as the man who embarrassed a member of the royal family or the soiling of the white linen tablecloth. It may not be so minor. Courts which find themselves having to deal with neighbor disputes often give them quick attention. Although judges wish neighbors would settle their disputes and not waste court time, judges recognize that quite often neighbor disputes may fester and give rise to violence.

What then should you do? This very common problem is one where damage has been done and therefore admits of application of some of the same research findings we considered earlier.

Unfortunately most persons whose dogs, for example, mess their neighbor's lawn try to escape embarrassment by hoping their dog will not be blamed. It is hard to prove your dog was responsible. Still your neighbor suspects it was your dog. He gets especially angry when he has to clean it up as he mutters to himself that it is bad enough that the dog has done damage to the lawn.

If this is a habit of your dog and you do not want to keep him on a leash or take him out, then keep an eye open for any evidence that your dog has made a deposit on the lawn. When that happens, be ready to do penance.

This means that you get busy with a shovel and bag or pooperscooper and simply clean it up. If the problem is urine, then a quick dousing with a water can will help. It is important, following the concept of doing penance, to act publicly and visibly to make it clear to your neighbor what you are doing. Act quickly then without trying to hide what you are doing. That gesture is not because you want to prove anything but because you recognize matter-of-factly that such things happen and you take full responsibility for it. Your neighbor will still probably wish you did not have a dog or would take closer care. At least he can see you accept the liability and are big enough to do what is necessary.

THE EARLY GUEST

Dinner has been set for eight. At 7:30, you and your co-host or co-hostess are dashing around, snatching up a week's accumulation of newspapers, hiding dirty dishes in the bottom cupboard, rushing for a quick shave and shower, when the doorbell rings. "Get it," your co-host or co-hostess shouts and you are indeed about to get it. For when you open the door there he stands with a bright smile on his face:

I wanted to give myself plenty of time to get here so I'm a bit early. (Ha Ha).

Try not to look unhappy by putting on a very happy face yourself to cover your irritation. Do a total reverse and reach out and seize his hand in an unmistakable gesture of welcome. "Bill!," you must shout, "Come right in!" (Then to your co-host or co-hostess, to make sure s/he knows since s/he may come marching out in a state of semi-nudity, "It's Bill, honey!").

Next, make two identity moves. First, recognize that you do have an entirely appropriate identity, namely that of the *host who is not ready*. After all it is only 7:35 and the appearance that would be wrong for 8:00 is quite right for 7:35. So it is quite appropriate that your hair is not combed or that you are unshaven, wearing a dirty T-shirt, or have a towel wrapped around you and that the house is also in a disordered state. Everything is precisely as it should be so do not apologize. It is he who has created a problem and he should be doing the apologizing if anybody should.

Second, alter his identity. In other words, put him to work repairing the damage he has caused by his early entry. He came early and deserves some punishment. Actually he will probably be feeling embarrassed and not be averse to being put to work. Have him put the peanuts out, get the liquor bottles ready or put out the glasses. You can even put a vacuum cleaner in his hand, if you are quick about it and do it as though you do not doubt for a minute that he will be willing to help. A good move is to suddenly snap your fingers as you say: "Thank goodness. We need help. I forgot to get the club soda (or mix or anything else that you can always use up). Let me get some money. I'd sure appreciate it if you would rush over to the supermarket and get some." He will be glad to do this favor, and if the supermarket is far enough away, by the time he returns, the other guests who will have arrived by then, will be wondering if he has forgotten to come to the party.

EMBARRASSED TO ASK FOR SOMETHING

Often big organizations manage to intimidate us because they know we do not want to make a fuss. Say you have been assigned a seat behind a pillar and you are not partial to white marble but you hesitate to ask for a better seat. Or you did not like a movie but do not quite have the nerve to ask for your money back or a ticket for another movie. You would like to buy that skirt but the price is really too high and you wish you could somehow get them to reduce it. In all these cases there is embarrassment which follows from our unwillingness to abase ourselves to ask for favors. We feel a bit like a beggar.

For some persons assertiveness training may help especially if the situation is one where you are being deprived of your rights. One problem with such training is that it sometimes urges people to get aggressive with the result that you might just get slapped in the face. Still if this is a frequent problem with you, you might want to try such training.

A second idea follows from experiments by sociologist Harold Garfinkel who had his students go to department stores and ask for reduction of the price on low-priced items. Although some students were too frightened to try, those that did found that, to their amazement, it worked in a surprising number of cases. After discovering this, much of their initial squeamishness vanished and they got good at it.

You might follow their example and *force* yourself to act. For example, ask for your money back at the movie house even though you feel you will not get anywhere. If you are polite, you may be surprised at the response. The management does want satisfied customers. More important, practice helps as Garfinkel's students found. You will get less reluctant after you try.

If you are not up that approach, then you might try to change the meaning of the act. If you feel that you are just acting like a beggar, then give a positive sense to the role of beggar.

The clue comes from the Yiddish word for beggar, *schnorrer*. This character has a long history in Yiddish literature. Originally he felt embarrassed at having to beg. Then he heard that giving charity was a noble act which the truly observant person should be glad to do as an expression of upright character. After the beggar had thought that one through, he developed a rhetoric in which he recognized that, in begging, he was giving the other person an opportunity to carry out a holy act. He therefore was unembarrassed to act since he was really conferring a benefit on the other.

Although I have presented the argument a bit tongue-in-cheek, I think there is a point in it. In asking, say, for a better seat at a public performance with assigned seats, you can turn things around and see yourself as giving the management a chance to confer a benefit on you. Say to your partner:

> I'll bet the cashier was really not thinking when she gave us these seats. She may be concerned to hear of our distress and be willing to do something about it. Let's give her an opportunity to try.

I have actually done this and though it does not always work, if there still are unassigned seats, it is often easy to get your seats changed. After doing so, I find myself feeling good about myself as well as feeling the cashier probably feels she helped create a better attitude toward the management.

This kind of approach often applies to other encounters with big organizations such as returning purchases or finding something you have bought does not work. Too many people simply accept what they are given as part of the price of living in a society dominated by large organizations. Being too embarrassed to act does not do you any good of course. But it also does not do corporations any good either. They have an unhappy customer who will probably not buy again and may pass the word around as well. At least it is worth giving the corporation a chance to correct a mistake. The officials may even thank you for your efforts. They will at least apologize.

HANDLING EMBARRASSING PUBLIC ACCUSATIONS

There are times you are in charge of a meeting when someone hurls an accusation of improper behavior or service at you. You may be able to defend the act easily enough but the problem is that others are present, perhaps even newspaper reporters, and your answer must somehow satisfy them as well. If you get flustered and turn red with embarrassment, your explanation, however satisfactory it might be, leaves persons feeling you were not really on top of your job.

The approach I suggest is to turn the tables so that the questioner is the person who feels embarrassed. This may seem unfair but I am not suggesting you browbeat the person or sneer at his question. What he should have done was consult you privately when you could respond comfortably. By a public accusation, he has put you on the spot and you have a right to defend yourself. That right is especially strong if you are speaking as chairperson or representative of some group. As their agent, you have a duty to defend them as well.

Here is a case told to me by a school superintendent in Oregon. At a public meeting, a member of the audience stood up and gave a broadside attack on the school administration. He simply said he was "sick and tired" of the waste of taxpayer money and wished a "better class of people" could be chosen for their jobs.

At another meeting, a questioner accused the administrators of taking their wives to a convention at taxpayer expense. The accuser had been in the city where the convention had been held and had accidentally run into several of the wives at the airport. The superintendent asked me how he could have handled these encounters. If you are in such a position, here are some ideas.

There has been some scientific work on the whole question of handling criticism. Although that work deals with person to person criticism rather than public gatherings, we can draw some clues from the research. Social psychologists James P. Curran and Peter M. Monti make a distinction between manipulative or aggressive criticism and assertive criticism. An aggressive critic acts like the questioner in the first case: he attacks the superintendent directly rather than anything he has done. Researchers Curran and Monti suggest asking for specific details. The superintendent might reply:

> You say we are wasting taxpayer money. Every administrator I know is opposed to that. What specifically do you have in mind? We have a budget of $114 million with hundreds of items. If you can nail down your concern, I want to hear about it.

Now comes the clincher. The problem is that the accusation is public. Therefore, I suggest you take steps to move the accusation to a private place. You might try:

> I can get a copy of our budget for us to look at. Please see me right after the meeting and we can arrange to go into whatever is on your mind. Now I want to move on to the next agenda item.

The second questioner made a different criticism. His was of the specific act of taking wives to the convention presumably at taxpayer expense. This kind of criticism is an example of what Curran and Monti call assertive. It should be met, they suggest, by asking the person to expand on it, to clarify, elaborate and present supporting evidence.

Again I suggest moving from a public to a private place. After expressions of appropriate skepticism or outright denial (if appropriate), you might say something like the following to the questioner:

> If you still think you have some reason to believe this, I want to see you right after the meeting. You have made a serious accusation, maybe even one legally actionable. Those you accuse must, I am sure you agree, have the right to defend themselves. No one here would want their names to be bandied about until they have that chance.

> Until I can meet with you, I want to assure you and everyone in this room of how seriously I take such a charge. If there is even a smidgen of substance to what you say, then whoever is responsible will have to answer to me. Next question.

I doubt there will be a next question. In this way you avoid a public argument which rarely solves any problems or makes anyone happy except those who enjoy a public fight. As a responsible person, you are under no obligation to provide such entertainment.

PART IV

Embarrassment:
The Most Human of Emotions

Embarrassment turns out to be a wondrous complex thing. From children's play to corporate failings, from everyday experiences as we walk down a busy street to the most exotic of cultures, things can go wrong leading everyone to feel embarrassed.

We have seen that powerful strategies can help manage it. Preventing, hiding, reducing significance, reinterpreting, transforming identities and social moves all have their uses. Still no matter how well the strategies work, embarrassment is ever lurking as a potential with each new situation that comes up.

That makes it sound rather grim but as we know, embarrassment is very often so much fun. In the final chapter we will ask why that is so. The simple answer is that embarrassment reminds everyone, even the most exalted of their common humanity. When the contrast between lofty pretensions and humble reality is exposed suddenly, as it often is in embarrassment, we are brought face to face with the comedy of everyday life.

Chapter 12

Enjoying Embarrassment

As painful as embarrassment can be, it is often funny, at least when it happens to someone else. Does this mean we are sadists at heart who enjoy witnessing the suffering of others? That cannot be the explanation. If that were true, how would we then explain how uncomfortable we feel when a performer or speaker is having trouble carrying on? Nor would such a dismal view of human nature explain those occasions when we leap to help someone who is blushing for having dropped several parcels, someone who sits on a chair which then collapses or someone who fumbles for a word.

We get a clue by looking at the classic cartoon figure of the man in a top hat who slips on a banana peel. We laugh at the tripping up of his false dignity. He is putting on airs and just because he is so concerned with his self importance, he forgets that his body is no different than ours, that he can slip in just the same way as the lowliest person on earth.

Like the top hatted figure, many persons walk the earth as privileged little deities, mindful only of their precious selves. When they become embarrassed, they are pulled off their high horses and shown to be like everyone else. We will laugh unless of course the person seems hurt a little too much. Our enjoyment does not necessarily betoken a sense of superiority. We are simply experiencing the good feeling we get when the basic equality among humans has in a small way been reaffirmed. Things have been set to right again and we feel a bit better at discovering there is some order in the world after all.

Yet we do not have to wait for persons to fall off their high horses. There are institutions and practices that seem to be found world-wide that make sure those who are or act superior remember that they are still human after all. What makes these practices interesting is that they can be such fun.

GETTING BACK AT SUPERIORS

One of the best places to find persons who get carried away with an exaggerated sense of their own importance is the modern bureaucracy. When you enter to confront the lofty officials behind the counter who look at you as if you were wasting their time, you feel put down immediately.

We can therefore readily understand (and secretly applaud) the woman who decided to express her opinion of the company by sitting on the new office photo-copying machine and allowing the machine to print up copies of her rear-end. The gesture by the way, is very common among rural peoples in several cultures. There a woman, especially if behind a window or in the back of a passing truck, may express her contempt for irreverent or hooting males by turning and flipping her skirt up to reveal her backside.

Ancient writers occasionally comment on the power of slaves to embarrass their masters by simply dragging their feet in banquet preparations when their masters most wanted to impress important guests. The practice is not rare in modern corporations either.

We have a weapon that the weakest persons in society can use since their superiors' ability to act superior depends on their services. Sociologist Thomas J. Scheff reports on a study of the power of mental hospital attendants to sabotage any program of group therapy by simply failing to round up patients for therapy sessions. Embarrassed psychiatrists then had to go hunting for their patients themselves. To get back at a particularly oppressive psychiatrist, attendants would urge patients to be ready to accost him the moment he arrived in the ward. The results were practically mob scenes from which the psychiatrist was grateful to be rescued.

Sometimes persons of low status do not dare confront their oppressors directly but content themselves with silent put-downs that only they are aware of (or they think so). The child who waits until the teacher's back is turned to stick out her tongue (to the accompaniment of giggles from fellow classmates) or the army private who shifts to the "four finger salute" (putting thumb to nose and wiggling the fingers back and forth) might appreciate the following research report of sociologist Marcia Millman.

Millman studied the activities of orderlies, maids, clean-up staff and other low-status personnel on the night shift of a private, university-affiliated hospital. After visiting hours are over and the hospital abandoned by the higher staff, a different mood comes over the hospital.

Status distinctions are reduced and rules relaxed. An orderly would visit around staff lounges and nurses' stations to report progress on a sportscar he was building from a kit. Another orderly violated the rules by playing his radio continually as he worked. Other low status workers stretched out where they pleased, spread out their lunches on usually forbidden places as they put up their feet on the desks of their lords and masters. Policemen, who stopped to visit awhile after bringing in an emergency patient, would bring in a pizza which was then sliced with surgical scalpels.

Millman calls all this "The Revenge of the Nightworkers." Although the daytime staff do not know their authority is being mocked (except perhaps when they wonder about a banana peel left on top of a word processor), the night-time staff takes some comfort from doing it in secret.

ROASTS

Although made popular by recent and much watered-down versions, the roast of a prominent public figure goes back at least to the 18th century in Great Britain. According to culture historian George A. Test, the roast in essentially present-day form made its first appearance in America in the founding of the Clover Club in Philadelphia on January 19, 1882. It described itself as a "Club for Social Enjoyments, the Cultivation of Literary Tastes and the Encouragement of Hospitable Intercourse."

The description fools no one. From the start the members get down to the real business of the evening which is to needle and showing irreverence to all speakers. The response appears to be spontaneous as the president wears out his gavel trying to keep order. The object, as Test puts it, is that derision and mockery have the effect that persons of:

"power and prominence (shall be) brought low and the quipper elevated by his wit and humor."

The Friars Club roasts are much better known because they include persons from the entertainment world. The guest of honor is one at the very height of his or her fame so that the occasion is both an honor and reminder of how fleeting fame can be. Although the roasts are full of embarrassing stories about the

206

roastee, they are also disguised compliments as, when George M. Cohan was roasted in 1910, the audience was invited to become a jury to try Cohan and find him guilty of being the "possessor of super skill in everything he undertakes." At the same time, he was continually put down as merely "Jesse Cohan's son," Jesse Cohan being present and a stage performer himself.

A similar process was evident at a more recent roast of Senator Throm Thurmond of South Carolina at a "Fall Guy" show, an event which has been going on for over 30 years. Jokes were made about the contrast of 45 years in ages between Senator Thurmond and his wife, Nancy with whom he has four children. A former secretary of the Navy spoke of once being a neighbor of the Thurmonds:

> Strom had a new pacemaker and every time he put his arm around Nancy, my garage doors would go up.

The Secretary was careful to balance his remarks with positive comments such as:

> Strom fights for principles we all believe in.

Roastees are supposed to take it in good humor as John F. Kennedy did before the Gridiron Club, a Washington club that specializes in roasting politicians. At the time (1958) he was running for the presidency. The grilling dwelt on his father's wealth. In a responding speech, John Kennedy said:

> I have just received the following wire from my generous Daddy. "Dear Jack: Don't buy a single vote more than necessary. I'll be damned if I'm going to pay for a landslide."

Although it is all supposed to be in good fun, there is evidence that the subject of the roast does not always enjoy it and that some of the satire cuts a bit too close to the bone to be amusing. President William Howard Taft wrote that, though the Gridiron dinners furnish much fun, still:

> After some training, both as Secretary of War and as President, I was able to smile broadly at a caustic joke at my expense and seem to enjoy it, with the consolatory thought that every other guest of any prominence had to suffer the same penalty for an evening's pleasure.

With respect I differ with the President. He and others of prominence are not supposed to enjoy themselves. Its goals, as Chauncey Depew, an original member of the Gridiron Club put it is to reveal:

> ...the statesman to himself as he is (and so)to reduce the abnormal swelling of the head and the enlargement of the chest.

The person roasted is in fact a ritual sacrifice, a modern representative of a practice known throughout the world. In the West it goes back to the Roman Saturnalia or the Feast of Fools of the middle ages when the lower clergy elected officers, delivered mock sermons and upturned the mass. The practice shows up in weakened forms in spoofs by students of their professors, or Esquire Magazine's annual "Dubious Achievement Awards" where some recent winners included a major league baseball player with the lowest batting average and certain manufacturers responsible for designer-label chocolates.

Strong or weak, the practice of subjecting prominent persons to public embarrassments when they must suffer through them and prove themselves "'good sports" is not likely to vanish. In current times, when men and women of influence are isolated by bureaucratic barriers from reminders of their humanity, such criticism seems hardly out of date.

BE A CLOWN

In princely courts of the middle ages the most absolute of tyrants surrounded themselves with royal buffoons who were allowed or even expected to ridicule the nobles or embarrass the prince himself. Far from threatening their power (although occasionally a fool went too far and literally lost his head), tryrants saw their fools as serving an essential function of unmasking fraud and pointing to weaknesses in the official claims of the nobility. The story of the emperor's new clothes shows how useful even a very young fool, an untutored child, might be in awakening a monarch to how much he had been duped by his tailors.

The adult fool had to be skilled and polished for he was dealing with sacred practices and high status persons. Therefore a direct criticism was dangerous. The fool had to clothe his criticism in clever verse, in song and satire or in some form which gave it grace and provided amusement. The fool would be saying to his target:

You are pompous but your pomposity is so funny that I know you can't really mean it.

209

The fool therefore will exaggerate the pomposity and with the smile of recognition, the target expresses agreement and solidarity.

Some persons play the fool quite deliberately in order to escape the high expectations of normal persons. Claudius, a member of the royal family in imperial Rome was able to pass himself off as a simpleton (made more credible by a bad stammer). Since he was regarded as no serious contender for the throne, he escaped plotting or possible assassination by rivals to live to become one of the great Roman emperors.

Former President Ronald Reagan would occasionally play a jester role as when he would feign having slept through a conference. Making a joke on his own age, I recall his once claiming that he had discussed some matter with President Lincoln but could not recall what he said. Because of his polish as a speaker and his training as an actor, Reagan was able to carry this pose off so winningly that most were prepared to forgive him, considering him all the more attractive for admitting to his faults.

One of the most endearing of all fools is known by the Yiddish word *schlemiel*, a butterfingers who fails in everything he tries but who never stops trying. In a serious study of this character, writer Enid Welsford defined him as:

> a man who falls below the average human standard but whose defects have been transformed into a source of delight.

For example, before a battle, a captain called his men together telling them they were going to charge the enemy to show who's boss. He said:

> It'll be man to man in hand to hand combat!

In the company there was an unwilling draftee with little stomach for the war. He called out:

> Please sir, show me my man. Maybe I can work out a deal with him.

In such a story the *schlemiel* shows both a fool's weakness but also a basic strength, a person who is outrageous and absurd in his innocence. In spite of what the world does to you, says the *schlemiel*, you have to keep your faith and keep trying.

In his stories of the ebullient Hyman Kaplan, Leo Rosten describes how Kaplan fairly glories in his many mistakes in his evening class for immigrants. When he makes those errors, others in the class are quick to point them out. With each correction, Kaplan, instead of being downcast, becomes increasingly pleased with himself. Who, he thinks, but a very remarkable person who has sought to express deep and complex ideas would make so many errors? The others merely make little slips. His mistakes are wonders of creative misunderstanding that leave his long suffering teacher gasping.

We do not have to limit ourselves to fiction to find examples of *schlemiels*. Stephen Pile describes the career of Thomas Nuttall, a pioneer explorer-botanist (1786-1859) who pushed into the unknown parts of northwest America. He had one flaw. He was almost always lost. On one occasion, his fellow explorers had to light beacons to help him find his way back.

> One night he completely failed to return and a search party was sent out. As it approached him in the darkness Nuttall assumed they were (hostile) Indians and tried to escape. The annoyed rescuers pursued him for three days through bush and river until he accidentally wandered back into camp.

211

Mr. Nuttall's case is not unique:

In 1972 Mr. J. Egan from London stole a barge on the River Thames and was very soon caught. There was a dock strike on and his was the only craft moving that day.

Writing of his own *schlemiel* "Herzog," in mind, Nobel prizewinning novelist Saul Bellow wrote that perhaps *schlemiels* were really quite common, a bit of them in all of us:

We must make what we can of our condition with the means available. We must accept the mixture as we find it–the impurity of it, the tragedy of it, the hope of it.

The next time you are in a bookstore, look over the section on "how to be successful," usually under "self help." There you find literally hundreds of such books ranging from dress, business, investments, marriage, sex, parenting, writing job resumes, dog grooming, cooking, sports and many others. The lesson to be learned from the sheer number of such books is not simply that people have an urge to be successful. Rather the lesson must be that most people are *not*.

As average humans, we make our way through life in a bumbling way. We do not walk straight but meander in a wavy line. We do adequately on the job and when we must we can cook a tolerable meal. Our clothes get wrinkled soon after being worn, we forget where we parked the car and when we do find it, discover we have locked the keys inside. We forget birthdays, are late for appointments and, on arrival, discover we did not bring along a needed document. We drink too much, eat too much, burp and are flatulent. In spite of all this we still think of ourselves as competent persons who deserve respect.

We *do* deserve respect not as superior beings but as humans. As Robert Louis Stevenson put it:

> Our business in life is not to succeed but to fail in good spirits.

That is not easy especially in a culture which emphasizes success as much as ours does, but we can try. If there is no fool around to poke holes in our pretensions, most of us get along quite well without him by making fools of ourselves. All of which is to say that we are going to be embarrassed a lot of the time.

BEING NATURAL

Today we are often urged to be ourselves, authentic and natural. We have grown tired of artificiality in clothes, ideas and government. We have been fooled and conned so many times that we yearn for honesty, for the nonpolitical politician, the straight answer, the bottom line. It is therefore not surprising that the ultimate therapy for bruised psyches and confused souls is said to be that of helping persons to get in touch with their true feelings, get their heads together or find ways to be cool.

While the urge to self expression can be marvelous in liberating us from unexamined prejudices, we are not given license to attack everything that displeases us or causes us discomfort. One of the things that some leaders of the human expression movement distrust is embarrassment. They claim it is a way of hiding your true feelings. Persons are urged not be embarrassed but to "let it all hang out."

One of the founders of Gestalt therapy, Fritz Perls, saw all forms of repression and self-constraint as the "enemy." Using a metaphor from World War 11, he called embarrassment a "Quisling," using the name of a disloyal Norwegian leader who acted as Hitler's puppet in assisting the Nazis:

> As the Quislings identify themselves with the enemy and not with their own people, so shame, embarrassment, selfconsciousness and fear restrict the individual's expressions. Expressions change into repressions.

I cannot comment on shame, self-consciousness and fear but as for embarrassment, I would agree that there are many things about which we should not feel embarrassed. We should not be too embarrassed to tell our doctor our symptoms or worries, nor to tell our lawyer everything he or she needs to know to represent us well. Therefore I would agree with Perls who was, after all, a therapist that persons should not feel too embarrassed to tell him about their secret longings and fears. But as a general program for living in the world, I think his advice is mistaken and for this reason.

It is certainly human and natural to feel fear, to hate persons, to get upset, to feel superior, to be jealous, to have cruel thoughts, to be vain, shy or boastful, to envy others and to have evil thoughts. But it is *also* quite natural to be embarrassed about feeling any of those emotions. Being authentic and true to yourself also includes, quite often, allowing yourself to be embarrassed. To try to deny it to yourself is really denying your own humanity.

In the 19th century, a great debate raged over whether Negroes (as they were called then) and American Indians (as they were called then) blushed or not. Because of differences in skin color, it was not obvious to the casual observer. British literary critic Christopher Ricks tells us that this was:

> ...not just foolishness or pedantry since it was involved in a sense of their full humanity.

It was a serious political question. Darwin had insisted that only humans blushed. Therefore if it could be shown that Negroes and American Indians did not blush (as white persons did), then that would place them in the same class as lower animals who could then be conquered and locked up at will. The debate over whether you were capable of blushing or not became part of the search for a justification for imperialism and slavery. To be able to blush was proof of your being entitled to basic human rights. And of course, as we showed in early chapters, African Americans and Native Americans do blush although we hardly think any more that that is proof of entitlement to human rights.

Another powerful reason why blushing and getting embarrassed is desirable was revealed in a simple experiment by British social psychologists Gun R. Semin and A. S. R. Manstead. Persons were shown videotapes in which a shopper "accidentally" knocks over a tier of toilet paper rolls with his cart. In one tape, he quickly set the rolls up again, in a second tape he left them. In one of the tapes he also showed embarrassment. In the other he did not. Persons who viewed the tapes were asked what they thought of the shopper.

The major finding was that they thought the shopper who rebuilt the display was mature and reliable. But they found the one who showed embarrassment more likeable.

The finding is hardly surprising. To show others you are embarrassed at some flub is to admit you can make mistakes just like they can. Another study showed that this effect is especially likely if the person who goofs is a superior person. It brings him down to his common humanity with the rest of us, as was shown in a surprising response to a celebrated singer's lapse of memory. In a performance in London, England, Richard Harris, who had sung the role of King Arthur in the musical *Camelot* a great many times, forgot the words to the song "What Do The Simple Folk Do?" Halfway through he suddenly stopped, waved to the orchestra for silence, then turned to the audience saying:

> Four hundred and twenty eight performances, and I have forgotten the lyrics. Would you believe it?

According to the London evening newspaper, *The Standard*, the admission earned for Harris the longest applause of the evening. Of course the audience was also delighted to be present when such a superstar goofed. They were even more delighted that he could admit the goof and still go on.

WHAT TO DO WHEN NOTHING WORKS

We have reviewed many ways of dealing with embarrassment. We can hide it, overlook it, make light of it, change its meaning, transform our identity and try for social moves to get others to change their opinions of our behavior.

When all those strategies fail, there remains one last weapon. You can simply admit it as Richard Harris did. Alternatively, since you are probably blushing or showing other signs of embarrassment, you can let those signs do their work. For those signs show not merely that you have flubbed or failed. That is obvious to anyone present .

Instead, you are making it clear that the failure is not shameful. Nor does it show any defect of character. All that has happened is that the self that has done the deed is not the self of which you are capable.

For the embarrassing event has only been a lapse. Once you get past it, persons will see they can count on you once more as they have in the past. In addition in discovering you *can* get past the embarrassment, you know you merit their faith that you can keep doing so. What is more, once you realize you do merit their trust, your ability to handle each new embarrassment as it comes up will get better each time you try.

References and Comments

CHAPTER 1:
EMBARRASSING MOMENTS—THEY HAPPEN TO EVERYONE

12.   Chinese philosopher Mencius' concern about embarrassing others is cited in Barrington Moore, Jr., *Privacy: Studies in Social and Cultural History*, Armonk, NY: M. E. Sharpe, 1984, p. 262.

Embarrassments in other countries and cultures have not been pulled together systematically. A general treatment of related topics can be found in the massive volume by Irenaus Eibl-Eibesfeldt, *Human Ethology*, New York: Aldine De Gruyter, 1989. Eibl-Eibesfeldt deals directly with embarrassment in his earlier work "Similarities and Differences Between Cultures in Expressive Movements," in R. A. Hinde (ed.), *Non-Verbal Communication*, Cambridge: Cambridge University Press, 1972, Chap. 11 (with excellent photographs). Also worth consulting is *The Body Reader: Social Aspects of the Human Body*. Ted Polhemus (ed.) New York: Pantheon, 1978.

The concept of "face" among the Chinese is carefully treated in David Yau-Fai Ho, "On the Concept of Face," *American Journal of Sociology* 81, 1976, 867-884. See also H. W. Smith, " A Modest Test of Cross-Cultural Differences in Sexual Modesty, Embarrassment and Self-Disclosure," *Qualitative Sociology*, 3, 1980, 233-241.

European and other variations are reported in papers by Robert J. Edelmann and associates in, for example, *The International Journal of Psychology*, 24, 1989, 351-366 or *Psychologia*. 30, 1987, 206-216.

The Balinese concern with *faux pas* which anthropologist Clifford Geertz renders as "stage fright" is discussed by him in "Person, Time and Conduct In Bali," *The Interpretation of Cultures*, New York: Basic Books, 1973, Chap. 14.

13.   The William the Conqueror story is told by British historian Edward S. Creasy in *The Fifteen Decisive Battles of the World*, New York: Harper (first published in 1851 but reprinted later with more battles added. I made

use of the 1872 edition.). Creasy credits the story to "the old Norman chroniclers."

13.   The report on embarrassment in children is summarized in Arnold M. Buss, *Self-Consciousness and Anxiety*, San Francisco, W.H. Freeman, 1980, pp. 237-240. See also Arnold M. Buss, Ira Iscoe and Edith H. Buss, "The Development of Embarrassment," *Journal of Psychology*, 103, 1979, 227-230.

The Buss studies asked parents when they first observed embarrassment in their children. In contrast, education researchers Laura Beizer Seidner, Deborah J. Stipek and Norma Deitch Feshbach actually interviewed 109 children in kindergarten, 2nd, 4th and 6th grades. Although the researchers refer to hints of embarrassment as early as the second year, two-thirds of the kindergartners (average age 5) were able to recount an embarrassing event. By the 2nd grade, the percentage rose to 80 and by 4th grade to over 95. See "A Developmental Analysis of Elementary School-Aged Children's Concepts of Pride and Embarrassment," *Child Development*, 59,1988, 367-377.

13-14. The Isabelle Leeds story is reported in the *St. Louis Post-Dispatch*, Jan. 13, 1980.

15.   Psychologist Jerome Sattler's study is "A Theoretical, Developmental, and Clinical Investigation of Embarrassment", *Genetic Psychology Monographs*, 71, 1959, 19-65. His adolescent sample was drawn from an 8th grade Topeka, Kansas school, his college sample from the University of Kansas and his "normal" adult sample from wives of hospital professional staff, secretaries and members of a civic club.

16.   The report on the United States Supreme Court is from *The Brethren* by Robert Woodward and Scott Armstrong, New York: Simon and Schuster, 1979, pp. 314 ff. The quotation is on p. 315.

16-17. The Roy Riegels misfortune has become part of football lore but it actually happened, as described in detail in John McCallum and Charles H. Pearson (eds.), *College Football U.S. A.* New York: Hall of Fame Publishers and McGraw-Hill, 1973, pp. 215-219.

17.   Chancellor Willy Brandt's troubles were reported in *Parade Magazine*, March 20,1980.

17-18. The beginning of the trial of Clark Clifford's associate, Robert Altman, is described in the *New York Times* of March 31, 1993. (Mr. Clifford was undergoing heart surgery).

18.   The NBC News apparent staging of the General Motors trucks crash is detailed in, among other places, *The Washington Post* (national weekly edition) for March 8-14, 1993.

19.   The Murphy bed case was presented in the *Seattle Post-Intelligencer*, May 11, 1980.

        Miss Manners' advice appeared in her syndicated column in the *Seattle Times*, Jan. 30, 1980.

21.   Secretary of War Profumo's escapades have been the subject of many reports. I got mine from Clive Irving, Ron Hall and Jeremy Wallington, *Anatomy of A Scandal*, New York: M. S. Mill and William Morrow, 1963. The quotation is from Profumo's letter of resignation on p. 138.

        The scandal of the 1919 World Series is laid out in detail in Eliot Asinof's *Eight Men Out*, New York: Holt, Rinehart and Winston, 1963. See also his *Bleeding Between the Lines*, New York: Holt, Rinehart and Winston, 1979.

22.   The story of Queen Victoria and the Empress of Japan has been told to me orally several times by reputable historians but I have been unable to find documentation.

        Beatrice Lillie's encounter with the pigeon is described in slightly varied words in several places. See Kenneth Tynan, Kathleen Tynan and and Ernie Eban, (eds.), *Profiles*, London: Hern, 1989, p. 112.

        The Leo Slezak story is told by his son, actor Walter Slezak in *What Time's The Next Swan?* New York: Doubleday, 1962.

22-23. This is the first of embarrassments I must confess. I wrote down the wonderful quotation from Senator Margaret Chase Smith when I first read it. Unfortunately I forgot to note the source and cannot find it.

23. The howlers from newspaper accounts can be found in Louis Untermeyer's classic collection, *A Treasury of Laughter*, New York: Simon and Schuster, 1946, p. 601

CHAPTER 2:
WHY IS EMBARRASSMENT SO UPSETTING?

27. The Minnesota Orchestra report is from the *Minneapolis Tribune*. Aug. 8, 1979.

29. French President Giscard d'Estaing's problems are detailed in *Time Magazine*, June 2, 1980, pp. 43-44

31. Robert Edgerton's research on coping strategies of the mentally retarded is presented in his *The Cloak of Competence*, Berkeley: University of California Press, 1967.

32. On the zipper-fly report, Professor Jan Harold Brunvand, an urban folklorist and author of several books on urban legends wrote me that he has encountered variations of this story from several sources. He finds the stories told not by a first person witness but by a "friend of a friend."

I replied that the story was told me by the wife of a former graduate student who did his graduate research under my direction. She and my student served in low level positions in the United States foreign services. Since I know both of them well and have for many years, I simply cannot believe she made up the story. She provided too many details of the event, the date and place (which I have deliberately left out) to cast doubt on the story's credibility.

It is my belief that occasionally urban legends are based on some actual happening which is then taken up, embellished and rendered as a commentary on human foibles by others. In any case, it is a good story and does illustrate not just a human foible but the frailty of reputations and identities.

33. Dear Abby's advice on what to do about hotel fires appeared in her column of Jan. 19, 1981 in the *Seattle Times*.

34.   Edward S. Herold, "Contraceptive Embarrassment and Contraceptive Behavior Among Single Young Women, *Journal of Youth and Adolescence* 10,1981 , 233-242.

The Guttmacher Institute survey was widely reported, for example in the *New York Times*, April 15, 1993.

34-35   There are many studies on helping behavior. The study on reluctance to appear foolish in ambiguous situations is Russell D. Clark III and Larry E. Word, "Why Don't Bystanders Help? Because of Ambiguity?" *Journal of Personality and Social Psychology*, 24, 1972, 329-400.

The study on embarrassment at picking up a Tampax box is reviewed by Robert J. Edelmann, *The Psychology of Embarrassment*, New York: Wiley, 1987, p. 138. The study was carried out by Edelmann and associates who are listed as J. Harvey Childs, I. Kollock and C. Strain-Clark in the Journal of Social Psychology, 124, 1984, 353-354. A nearly identical study (except for use of a box of envelopes instead of a packet of tea) with nearly identical results was Nell C. Crenshaw and Robert D. Foss, "Risk of Embarrassment and Helping," *Social Behavior and Personality*, 6, 1978, 233-245.

35.   The arm-sling and knee brace study is Richard J. Pomazel and Gerald L. Clore, "Helping on the Highway: The Effects of Dependency and Sex," *Journal of Applied Social Psychology*, 3, 1973, 150-164.

The study of reluctance to help someone with a birthmark is by Irving M. Piliavin, Jane Allyn Piliavin and Judith Rodin, "Costs, Diffusion, and the Stigmatized Victim," *Journal of Personality and Social Psychology*, 32, 1975, 429-438.

The unwillingness of masculine types to help persons choking on a doughnut is described in Dianne M. Tice and Roy F. Baumeister, "Masculinity Inhibits Helping in Emergencies: Personality Does Predict the Bystander Effect," *Journal of Personality and Social Psychology*, 49, 1985, 420-428. They mention another study with different results but explain those as due to how the data were handled.

35.	There are many studies of how persons needing government help are inhibited from asking by embarrassment as well as other reasons. See John B. Williamson, "The Stigma of Public Dependency: A Comparison of Alternative Forms of Public Aid to the Poor," *Social Problems*, 22, 1974, 213-238. A general discussion of a lot of related research is by E. Gary Shapiro, "Help Seeking: Why People Don't," in *Research in the Sociology of Organizations*, 3, 1984, 213-236, and in another Shapiro paper: "Embarrassment and Help-Seeking," in Bella M. DePaulo, Arie Nadler and Jeffrey D. Fisher (eds.), *New Directions in Helping*, Vol. 2, New York: Academic Press, 1983, Chap. 6.

36.	Solomon Asch's classic experiments are described in his book, *Social Psychology*, Englewood Cliffs, NJ: Prentice-Hall, 1952, Chap. 16.

Stanley Milgram,*Obedience to Authority: An Experimental View*, New York: Harper and Row, 1974.

36-37.	George Orwell's vivid reports come from his own experience as published in *Shooting and Elephant and Other Essays*, New York: Harcourt Brace, 1950, pp. 8-9 and 12.

CHAPTER 3:
THE HIDDEN BLESSINGS OF EMBARRASSMENT

42-43. The physiological mechanisms that underlie embarrassment are not well understood as is the case for emotions generally. There is controversy on whether emotions are all based on the same neurological and hormonal basis or not. An equally controversial question is whether emotions are culture-specific or the same the world over. See for example, Peter Ekman and W. V. Friesen, *Unmasking the Face*, Englewood Cliffs, NJ: Prentice-Hall, 1975 and Theodore D. Kemper, *A Social Interactional Theory of Emotions*, New York: Wiley, 1978. Other sociological approaches to emotion are presented in Rom Harre', (ed.) *The Social Construction of Emotions*. Oxford: Basic Blackwell, 1981; Carolyn Saarni and Paul L. Harris (eds.) *Children's Understanding of Emotions*, New York: Cambridge University Press, 1989; and Thomas J. Scheff and Suzanne M. Retzinger, *Emotions and Violence*, Lexington, MA: Lexington Books, 1991.

The Desmond Morris reference is to *Manwatching*, New York: Harry N. Abrams, 1977, pp. 166-168. The photographs are superb.

44. Charles Darwin, *The Expression of the Emotions in Man and Animals*. London: William Pickering, 1989 (a reprinting of the second edition of 1890).The quotations are from p. 244. A neglected work that has influenced my thinking is John T. MacCurdy's, "The Significance of Blushing and Shame," *British Journal of Psychology* 71, 1965, 19-59.

45. Dermatalogical research findings are treated in Jonathan K. Wilkin, "Why Is Flushing Limited to a Mostly Facial Cutaneous Distribution?" *Journal of the Academy of Dermatology*, 19, 1988, 309-313 and Stephanie A. Shields, Mary E. Mallory and Angela Simon, "The Experience and Symptoms of Blushing as a Function of Age and Reported Frequency of Blushing," *Journal of Nonverbal Behavior*, 14, 1990, 171-187.

Chronic blushing findings are reported in Robert J. Edelmann, "Chronic Blushing, Self-Consciousness, and Social Anxiety," *Journal of Psychopathology and Behavioral Assessment,* 12, 1990, 119-127 and more generally in Edelmann's chapter in W. Ray Crozier (ed.) *Shyness and Embarrassment*, New York: Cambridge University Press, 1990, Chap. 7.

45. Mark R. Leary and Sarah Meadows, "Predictors, Elicitors and Concomitants of Social Blushing," *Journal of Personality and Social Psychology*, 60, 1991, 254-262.

45-46. Cristiano Castelfranchi and Isabella Poggi, "Blushing as Discourse: Was Darwin Wrong?" in W. Ray Crozier (ed.) *Shyness and Embarrassment*, New York: Cambridge University Press, 1990, Chap 8. Although they present their theory in terms of shame, I think their argument applies even more to embarrassment since blushing may be more common in embarrassment than in shame. The Leary-Meadows paper cited above also discusses this theory.

46. Eibl-Eibesfeldt's work has been cited earlier in footnotes to page 12 above.

225

48. Statistics on large organizations are drawn from Edward Gross and Amitai Etzioni, *Organizations in Society*, Englewood Cliffs, NJ: Prentice-Hall, 1985, Chap. 10.

49. Bill Bryson, Jr., *The Blook of Bunders*, New York: Dell, 1982, pp. 34-35.

The material on firemen's climbing ladders is one of many practices described by Thomas J. Matthews, "The Urban Fire Station: A Sociological Study of an Occupation," Unpublished M. A Thesis, Dept of Sociology, The State College of Washington (now known as Washington State University), 1950. For instance he describes the "smoke-eater" who, in a smoke-filled room, will take quick gulps of air from the hose before the water comes surging through. That is not one for the inexperienced to try.

49-50. Policemen's conduct has been studied by many researchers. My example is drawn from the research of Jonathan Rubinstein, *City Police*, New York: Farrrar Straus and Straus, 1972, pp. 302-317.

50-51. The *Washington Post* report appeared on April 16, 1981 and following issues. There are other reports, especially of political scandals many of which have been brought together by Suzanne Garment in *Scandal: The Crisis of Mistrust in American Politics*, New York: Times Books of Random House, 1991 .

51-52 Spoonerisms have entered the language by attribution. Clifton Fadiman *The Little, Brown Book of Anecdotes*, Boston: Little, Brown, 1985, p. 518) refers to those on p. 52 as "likely but probably apocryphal" stating that one of the "best attested" is "Kinquering congs their titles take."

52-54. Iona and Peter Opie, *The Lore and Language of School Children*, Clarenden Press, Oxford University, 1960.

54-56. The literature on verbal dueling is extensive. My quotes are from William Labov, *Language in the Inner City*, Philadelphia: University of Pennsylvania Press, 1972. Others include Edith A. Folb, *Runnin' Down Some Lines*, Cambridge, MA: Harvard University Press, 1980. and Mary Sanches and Ben G. Blount (eds.) *Sociocultural Dimensions of Language Use*, New York: Academic Press, 1975. Other more general works worth considering

226

include Muriel Saville-Troike, *The Ethnography of Communication*, Baltimore: University Park Press, 1982, esp. Chap. 3; Peter Burke and Roy Porter (eds.) *The Social History of Language*, New York: Cambridge University Press, 1987, esp. the material on insults, proverbs and quackery; and a theoretical work James Paul Gee, *The Social Mind*, New York: Bergin & Garvey, 1992.

57. The Kennedy story provides my second embarrassment. I read it and was so delighted with it that I forgot to write down the source. Now I wonder if perhaps it was simply attributed to President Kennedy since great stories often seem to find their way into the mouths of famous persons. It seems so characteristic that it is hard to believe he did not say it.

CHAPTER 4: THE CAUSES OF EMBARRASSMENT

59. On the general sociological theory of embarrassment, see the research in Edward Gross and Gregory P. Stone,"Embarrassment and the Analysis of Role Requirements," *American Journal of Sociology*, 70, 1964, 1-15. See also Erving Goffman, "Embarrassment and Social Organization," *American Journal of Sociology*, 62, 1956, 264-274. Works by psychologists include Barry R. Schlenker, *Impression Management*, Monterey: CA.: Brooks/Cole, 1980; James T. Tedeschi (ed.) *Impression Management Theory and Social Psychological Research*, New York: Academic Press, 1981; Robert J. Edelmann, *The Psychology of Embarrassment*, New York: Wiley, 1987 and W. Ray Crozier (ed.) *Shyness and Embarrassment*, New York: Cambridge University Press, 1990.

60. Ronald and Juliette Goldman, *Children's Sexual Thinking*, London, Routledge and Kegan Paul, 1982.

61. Andre Modigliani, "Embarrassment, Facework, and Eye Contact." *Journal of Personal and Social Psychology* 17, 1971, 15-24.

62-63 Jeffrey M. Jackson and Bibb Latané, " All Alone in Front of All Those People: Stage Fright as a Function of Number and Type of Co-Performers and Audience,"*Journal of Personality and Social Psychology*, 40, 1981, 73-75.

64.   Michael Shudson, "Embarrassment and Erving Goffman's Idea of Human Nature," *Theory and Society*, 13, 1984, 633-648.

The matter of embarrassability is not an all-or-nothing affair. Andre Modigliani ("Embarrassment and Embarrassability," *Sociometry*, 31, 1968, 313-326) found that persons high in empathic ability (sensitivity to others' feelings) were likely to be more embarrassable. How much self esteem one has is also important.

64-65. I have searched my files as well as biographies of King Edward Vll for his reply to his valet but do not find it. His biographers do agree that he was very keen on correct clothing. Leaving the bottom button on the vest unbuttoned is considered one of his contributions to fashion but may perhaps have been simply an adjustment to his ample figure. See Giles St. Aubyn, *Edward VII: Prince and King*, New York: Antheneum, 1979 and Christopher Hibbert, *Edward VII: A Portrait*, Lippincott, 1976, pp. 194-197.

65.   In a paper ("Embarrassment: A Dramaturgic Account," *Journal for the Theory of Social Behavior*, 17, 1987, 47-61), Maury Silver, John Sabini and W. Gerrod Parrott take me to task for claiming that embarrassment is surprising. Actually I do not make such a claim as you can see from the discussion on pages 65-66. I merely assert that it is sudden in discovery. Embarrassment might, of course, be surprising but it need not be as Silver and his colleagues correctly point out.

69.   This and following analyses are based on the Gross/Stone paper cited above for page 59.

70.   Arie Nadler, Rina Shapiro and Shulamit Ben-Itzhak, "Good Looks May Help: Effects of Helpers' Physical Attractiveness and Sex of Helper on Males' and Females' Help-Seeking Behavior," *Journal of Personality and Social Psychology*, 42, 1982, 90-99.

71.   The report on the embarrassed football player on the elevator is from Laurel Richardson, "'No, Thank You!': A Discourse on Etiquette," reprinted in Leonard Cargan and Jeanne. H. Ballantine (eds.), *Sociological Footprints*, Belmont, CA: Wadsworth, 1988, p. 87.

CHAPTER 5: SHYNESS AND SHAME

75. Distinctions are drawn between shyness, shame and embarrassment by Susan Shott, "Emotion and Social Life: A Symbolic Interactionist Analysis," *American Journal of Sociology*, 84, 1979, 317-1334. See also Bert R. Brown and Howard Garland, "The Effects of Incompetency, Audience Acquaintanceship and Anticipated Evaluative Feedback on Face-Saving Behavior," *Journal of Experimental Social Psychology*, 7, 1971, 490-502.

On shyness, see Philip G. Zimbardo, with Paul A Pilkonis and Margaret E. Marnell, *Shyness*, Reading, MA: Addison-Wesley, 1977, and, with Shirley L. Radl, *The Shy Child*, New York: McGraw-Hill, 1981. A recent summary is Warren H. Jones, *Shyness: Perspectives on Research and Treatment*, New York: Plenum, 1986.

The literature on shame is vast. An older book that I have found especially impressive is Helen M. Lynd, *Shame and the Search for Identity*, New York: Harcourt Brace, 1958. The French existentialist philosopher and dramatist Jean-Paul Sartre has dealt with shame in *Being and Nothingness*, New York: Philosophical Library, 1956 especially on pages 288 ff.

Psychoanalytic writers associate embarrassment with "erythrophobia" and "scotophilia" in, for example Otto Fenichel's classic, *The Psychoanalytic Theory of Neurosis*, New York: Norton, 1945 or Gerhard Piers and Milton B. Singer, *Shame and Guilt*, Springfield, IL: Charles C. Thomas, 1953.

A valuable treatment which insightfully deals with several theoretical positions is by theologian Carl D. Schneider, *Shame, Exposure and Privacy*, Boston: Beacon Press, 1977. In a class by itself is the brilliant treatment of the importance of embarrassment in both the life and poetry of Keats, Christopher Ricks, *Keats and Embarrassment*, London: Oxford Univerity Press, 1974.

The Leary/Schlenker work cited on p. 75 is: Mark R. Leary and Barry R. Schlenker, "The Social Psychology of Shyness: A Self-Presentational Model," in James T. Tedeschi (ed.), *Impression Management Theory and Social Psychological Research*, New York: Academic Press, 1981, Chap. 16.

76.   Secretary of State Haig's goof was reported in the *Seattle Post-Intelligencer*, Aug. 7, 1981.

76-77. The Clinton-Yeltsin embarrassment was reported in the *Seattle Post-Intelligencer*, April 6, 1993.

77.   Philip G. Zimbardo, *Shyness*, Reading, MA: Addison-Wesley, 1977.

78.   The quote on baritone Cornell MacNeill's problems with Rock Cornish hens is in Philip G. Zimbardo, *Shyness* (cited above), p. 28.

78-79. Mary K. Babcock and John Sabini, "On Differentiating Embarrassment from Shame," *European Journal of Social Psychology*, 20, 1990, 151-169.

        Some social scientists disagree with these distinctions preferring to see embarrassment as a variant of shame. See for example, Thomas J. Scheff and Suzanne M. Retzinger, *Emotions and Violence*, Lexinton, MA: Lexington Books, 1991.

80-81. The report of the bank robber who gave his identity away on the deposit slip is from Stephen Pile's *The Incomplete Book of Failures*, New York: Dutton, 1979.

81.   The "hirsutism" problem is discussed by syndicated columnist Doctor Coleman in a column dated Nov. 10,1979, *Seattle Post-Intelligencer*.

83.   The story of the Missouri basketball player who shot himself in the leg was reported in the *Seattle Post-Intelligencer*, Dec. 30, 1980. The experience of the pilot who landed at the wrong airport is from the same newspaper, June 22, 1980.

84-85   Robert Apsler, "Effects of Embarrassment on Behavior Toward Others," *Journal of Personality and Social Psychology*, 32, 1975, 145-153.

86.   Jerome Sattler's research is cited above for page 15.

        Mary K. Babcock, "Embarrassment: A Window on the Soul," *Journal for the Theory of Social Behavior.*" 18, 1988, 459-483.

87.   Douglas M. More, "Demotion," *Social Problems*, 9, 1962, 21 3-221.

87-88. Rosabeth Moss Kanter, *Men and Women of the Corporation*, New York: Basic Books, 1977.

88.   Burton R. Clark, "The Cooling-Out Function in Higher Education," *American Journal of Sociology*, 65, 1960, 569-576. Recent treatments are more skeptical about the success of community colleges in realizing some of the early hopes of its ability to redress inequality. See S. Brint and J. Karabel, *The Diverted Dream: Community Colleges and the Promise of Educational Opportunity in America*, 1900-1985, New York: Oxford University Press, 1989 and Dennis McGrath and Martin B. Spear, *The Academic Crisis of the Community College*, Albany: SUNY Press, 1991.

PART II: AVOIDING EMBARRASSMENT

91.   Senator Robert Kennedy's goof in Kenya is recounted in Art Linkletter's *Oops or Life's Awful Moments*, New York: Doubleday, 1967.

Conductor Jose Serebrier's self-surgery is reported in the *New York Times*, March 25, 1975.

CHAPTER 6: PREVENTION

93-94. General preventive moves are discussed in detail by Erving Goffman in several places but especially in an early paper, "On Face-Work," *Psychiatry*, 18, 1955, 213-221 and the following books: *Behavior in Public Places*, New York: Free Press of Glencoe, 1963; *Relations in Public*, New York: Harper and Row, 1971; and *Frame Analysis*, New York: Harper, 1974.

95.   The George Burns story is given in Clifton Fadiman (ed.) *The Little, Brown Book of Anecdotes*, Boston: Little, Brown, 1985, p. 88.

95-96. The lecture by Samuel C. Heilman in which he used the "salad" metaphor was given on April 22, 1993 at the University of Washington, Seattle.

98. The report of the Melbourne thieves originally appeared in a media report in 1966 as quoted in Erving Goffman, *Relations in Public,* Harper and Row, 1971, p. 308 from which I have the cited passage.

99-100. Ronald Wardhaugh, *How Conversation Works,* Oxford: Basic Blackwell, 1985, p. 2.

100. Erving Goffman, "Response Cries," in M. Von Cranach, K. Foppa, W. Lepenies and D. Ploog (eds.) *Human Ethology: Claims and Limits of a New Discipline,* Cambridge: Cambridge University Press, 1979, pp. 203-230.

100-101. Thomas J. Scheff, *Being Mentally Ill.* New York: Aldine, 1984. pp. 54-55.

101. The rational gestures of children in the classroom are examined in a paper of mine, Edward Gross, "The Rationality of Symbolic Actors," *British Journal of Sociology,* 38, 1987, 139-157.

102. Janey Levine, Ann Vinson and Deborah Wood, "Subway Behavior," in Arnold Birenbaum and Edward Sagarin (eds.) *People in Places,* New York: Praeger, 1973, pp. 208-216. The quotation is on p. 210.

103. Michael Wolff, "Notes on the Behavior of Pedestrians," in Arnold Birenbaum and Edward Sagarin (eds.)*People in Places,* cited above, pp. 122- 137.

103-104. Erving Goffman, *Behavior in Public Places,* New York: Free Press of Glencoe, 1963, pp. 83-88. The quotation is on p. 84.

104-105. David Givens, "Greeting A Stranger: Some Commonly Used Nonverbal Signals of Aversiveness," *Semiotica,* 22, 1978, 351 -367.

106. Glosses are discussed in Erving Goffman, *Relations in Public,* New York: Harper and Row, 1971, pp. 122- 137.

107. Rosabeth Moss Kanter, *Men and Women of the Corporation,* New York: Basic Books, 1977, Chap. 4. The quotation is on p. 80. In *Lying* (New York: Pantheon, 1978) Sissela Bok takes a dim view of lying in general. Protecting the boss may be covered by less harsh words On lying, various recent psychological studies are brought together in Michael

Lewis and Carolyn Saarni (eds.) *Lying and Deception in Everyday Life,* New York: Guilford Press, 1993.

108. Charlotte Green Schwartz, "Perspectives on Deviance—Wives' Definition of Their Husbands' Mental Illness," *Psychiatry,* 20, 1957, 275-291.

109. Art Linkletter's report on zipper-catching is from his *Oops or Life's Awful Moments,* New York: Doubleday, 1967.

CHAPTER 7: HIDING AND PRETENDING: CAN THEY WORK?

111. Thomas J. Scheff and Suzanne M. Retzinger, *Emotions and Violence,* Lexington, MA: Lexington Books, 1991, Chap. 3.

112. Quotation is from Scheff and Retzinger (cited above) p. 49.

112-113. Lawrence Langner, *The Importance of Wearing Clothes,* New York: Hastings House, 1959.

113. The report on the woman soldier in the Civil War is from her biography Madame Loreta Janeta Velaquez, *The Woman in Battle,* Richmond, VA.: Dustin, Gilman and Co., 1876, reprinted in 1972, edited by C. J. Worthington. Her experiences as well as those of other women are recounted in Richard Hall, *Patriots in Disguise: Women Warriors in the Civil War,* New York: Paragon House, 1993.

113-114. Daniel Albas and Cheryl Albas, "Aces and Bombers: The Post-Exam Impression Management Strategies of Students," *Symbolic Interaction,* 11, 1988, 289-302. The quotation is on p. 296.

115. Erving Goffman, *Stigma,* Englewood Cliffs, NJ: Prentice-Hall, 1963. The quotation is on p. 77.

116-117. Joseph W. Schneider and Peter Conrad, "In the Closet With Illness: Epilepsy, Stigma Potential and Information Control," *Social Problems,* 28, 1980, 32-44. The quotations on preventive telling are on p. 41.

116. The survey statistics on objections to employing epileptics are reported in Rigmor Jensen and Mogens Dam, "Public Attitudes Toward Epilepsy in Denmark," *Epilepsia*, 33, 1992, 459-463.

117. Dinsen's attempt to change his name to "Taxfighter" is reported in Rodney R. Jones and Gerald F. Uelmen's collection *Supreme Folly*, New York: Norton, 1990, p. 105

117. Leonard Broom, Helen B. Beem and Virginia Harris, "Characteristics of 1107 Petitioners for Change of Name," *American Sociological Review*, 20, 1955, 20-39. Quotation is on p. 39.

118. The couple who wanted to change their name from "Schitz" is mentioned in the *Seattle Post-Intelligencer*, Aug. 2, 1983.

Mary C. Waters, "The Everyday Use of Surname to Determine Ethnic Ancestry," *Qualitative Sociology*, 12, 1989, 303-324. The quotation is on p. 318.

The name changes in the Guggenheim family were chronicled in H. L. Mencken's *The American Language* from which Stanley Lieberson provided an extract from which I drew the names. Lieberson's article is:"What's in a Name?. . .Some Linguistic Possibilities," *International Journal of the Sociology of Language*, 45, 1984, 77-87.

119. The anecdote attributed to Maria Callas is given in Sir Rudolph Bing, *5000 Nights at the Opera*, Garden City: Doubleday, 1972, p. 231.

119-120. William F. Whyte, Jr., *Human Relations in the Restaurant Industry*, New York: McGraw-Hill, 1948, pp. 34 ff. The quotation from the sea-food supervisor is on p. 43.

121. Dan Sabbath and Mandel Hall, *End Product*, New York: Urizen Books, 1977. Quotation is on pp. 90-91

123. Barrington Moore, Jr., *Privacy: Studies in Social and Cultural History*, Armonk, NY: M. E. Sharpe, 1984.

124. Quotation from Barrington Moore, Jr., *Privacy*, cited above, p. 59.

234

125. Leon C. Metz, *Pat Garrett: The Story of a Western Lawman*, Normal, Okla.: University of Oklahoma Press, 1974.

127-128. Dumas Malone, *Jefferson and His Time, Vol. 2: Jefferson and the Rights of Man*, Boston: Little, Brown, 1951. The quotation on what the left hand might tell is on p. 73.

Charles van Pelt's recounting of events that may have caused the wrist fracture are in "Thomas Jefferson and Maria Cosway," *American Heritage*, 22, No. 5, Aug. 1971, p. 25.

PART III: MANAGING EMBARRASSMENT

129. John Austin, *Philosophical Papers*, Oxford: Oxford University Press, 1961, Chap. 6.

Works on excuses and other accounts include Erving Goffman, *Relations in Public*, New York: Harper, 1971, Chap. 4; Stanford Lyman and Marvin B. Scott, *A Sociology of the Absurd*, New York: Appleton-Century-Crofts, 1970, Chap. 5; Barry R. Schlenker, *Impression Management*, Monterey, CA.: Brooks/Cole, 1980, Chap. 5; C. R. Snyder, Raymond L. Higgins and Rita J. Stucky, *Excuses: Masquerades in Search of Grace*,New York: Wiley, 1983 and several chapters in Michael Lewis and Carolyn Saarni (eds.) *Lying and Deception in Everyday Life*, New York: Guilford Press, 1993; William F. Sharkley and Laura Stafford, "Responses to Embarrassment," *Human Communication Research*, 17, 1990, 315-342.

Popular treatments include Jerald M. Jellison, *I'm Sorry I Didn't Mean To And Other Lies We Love to Tell*, New York: Chatham Square, 1977 and Donald Carroll, *The Best Excuse. . .*New York: Coward-McCann, 1983.

130. Aviator Corrigan's memorable trip to Ireland is reported in the *New York Times*, July 19, 1938.

In *The Klutz Handbook*, Argus Communications, 1980, page 71, the author, Andrew David quotes the inspired past tense of "slide" by Dizzy

235

Dean. The quotation is stated to be from the *Reader's Digest*. No date is given.

The Yogi Berra quotation is cited in Ralph Keyes, *Nice Guys Finish Seventh*, New York: HarperCollins, 1992, p. 150 along with other famous Berraisms. Since Keyes is concerned in this book with tracing saying origins, he suggests this one may have been attributed to him by sportswriters.

131.   Former President Ford's problems are reviewed in Ron Nesson, *It Sure Looks Different From the Inside*, Chicago, Playboy Press, 1968, pp. 165 and 167.

A report of Ambassador Warren Austin's reputed goof is made in Richard Smith and Edward Dexter, *Oops: The Complete Book of Bloopers*. New York Rutledge, 1981, p. 112.

CHAPTER 8: REDUCING SIGNIFICANCE

133.   The Sir Thomas Beecham story was told to me by a British historian who could not recall where he had heard or read it. Perhaps Sir Thomas never said it but it is in keeping with his known character.

134.   The Dorothy Parker recovery from the looming embarrassment can be found in Andrew David, *The Klutz Handbook*, cited above pp. 37-38.

Winston Churchill's put-down of his detractors is quoted in Oscar Levant, *The Unimportance of Being Oscar*, New York: G. P. Putnam's, 1968, p. 205. No source is provided.

135.   Former President Ford's comeback remark was quoted in *Newsweek Magazine*, Jan. 1,1990, p. 44.

Lyndon B. Johnson's repartee with President de Gaulle is in William S. White, *The Professional: Lyndon B. Johnson*, Boston: Houghton Mifflin, 1964, p. 236. The Lincoln story is in Paul F. Boller, *Presidential Anecdotes*, New York: Oxford University Press, 1981, p. 125.

236

135-136   Versions of the story attributed to Dame Agatha may be found in several collections, e.g. *The Macmillan Dictionary of Quotations*, New York: Macmillian, 1987, p. 350; James B. Simpson, *Simpson's Contemporary Quotations*, Boston: Houghton Mifflin, 1988, p. 178.

136.   Larry Speakes' invention of the comment he attributed to President Reagan is recounted in John Whitcomb and Claire Whitcomb, *Great American Anecdotes*, New York: William Morrow, 1993, pp 208-209. They cite it as occurring in a PBS show, April 2, 1990.

144.   The advertisement for the Doberman was reported by columnist William Safire, reprinted in the *Seattle Post-Intelligencer*, Aug. 24, 1981.

The "probably improbable" forecast I heard on a TV broadcast interview but I regret I did not take the trouble to make a note of the date nor network source.

144-145. Kermit Shafer has printed and recorded many bloopers in *Pardon My Blooper*, Greenwich, Conn: Fawcett Crest Books, 1959 and *Prize Bloopers*, Greenwich, Conn: Fawcett Gold Medal Books 1965 and other places.

There are many other collections. A compilation edited by the Columbia Journalism Review and assembled by Gloria Cooper is entitled *Squad Helps Dog Bite Victim*, New York, Doubleday, 1980.

Comedian and talk-show host Jay Leno has compiled such headlines in several books. One example is *Headlines III: Not the Movie, Still the Book*, New York: Warner Books, 1991.

145.   Rose Laub Coser, "Some Social Functions of Laughter," *Human Relations*. 12, 171-182, 1959; "Laughter Among Colleagues: A Study of the Social Functions of Humor Among the Staff of a Mental Hospital," *Psychiatry*, 23, 81-95, 1960 and *Training in Ambiguity*, New York: Free Press, 1979.

145-146. Morris Rosenberg, *Conceiving the Self*, New York: Basic Books, 1954.

M. D. Lynch, "Self-Concept Development in Children," in M. D. Lynch, A.A. Norem-Hebeisen and K. Gergen (eds.) *Self-Concept: Advances in Theory and Research,* Cambridge: MA: Ballinger, 1981.

CHAPTER 9: CHANGING MEANINGS

151. The skittering hot-dog report is included in Carolyn Saarni, "Children's Understanding of Strategic Control of Emotional Expression in Social Transactions," in Carolyn Saarni and Paul L. Harris (eds.) *Children's Understanding of Emotion,* Cambridge: Cambridge University Press, 1989, Chap. 7.

151-152. President Eisenhower's attempt to redefine Sherman Adams' gifts is described in Herbert S. Parmet. *Eisenhower and the American Crusade,* New York: Macmillan, 1972, p. 522.

152. Candidate Richard Nixon's "Checkers" speech and the accompanying events are reported in Earl Mazo and Stephen Hess, *Nixon: A Political Portrait,* New York: Harper and Row, 1968, Chap. 9.

154. Gail Sheehy, *Passages,* New York: Dutton, 1976. Elizabeth Kubler-Ross, *On Death and Dying,* New York: Macmillan, 1969 and *Working It Through,* New York: Macmillan, 1982.

"Stage" theories are analyzed in John P. Hewitt and Peter M. Hall, "Social Problems, Problematic Situations and Quasi-Theories," *American Sociological Review.* 38, 1973, 369-374.

156. The actor Mel Gibson's interview was reported in the *Seattle Post-Intelligencer,* Sept. 1, 1981.

157. Former President Johnson's claim to birth in a shack is recounted in Hugh Sidey, *A Very Personal Presidency: Lyndon B. Johnson in the White House,* New York: Atheneum, 1968, p. 167.

Robert Benchley's comment to his wife is found in Nathaniel Benchley, *Robert Benchley,* New York: McGraw-Hill, 1955, p. 19.

158. I (along with millions of others) heard Ann Richards use the "silver foot in his mouth" metaphor at the Democratic party convention in 1992. Ralph Keyes (*Nice Guys Finish Seventh*, New York: HarperCollins, 1992 pp. 78-79) points out that others before Miss Richards had used the saying. As I note, she did not claim it was original.

166. Dale Carnegie's quote is in *How To Win Friends and Influence People*, New York: Simon and Schuster, 1964, p. 79.

167. The "Hoobert Heever" blooper has been told in many places. My source is a sound recording *Kermit Shaffer Presents. . . All Time Great Bloopers*, Blooper Enterprises, Inc., Vol. 1, Side 1. It is not clear whether the recording was made at the time or whether it is a re-enactment.

CHAPTER 10: MANAGING YOUR IDENTITIES

1 70-1 71. The exchange between pianist Godowsky and violinist Elman is given in Howard Taubman, *Music On My Beat*, New York: Simon and Schuster, 1943, p. 100. Taubman refers to the exchange as a "legend." I have also heard it of pianist Vladimir Horowitz and violinist Isaac Stern.

171. Law Professor Alan M. Dershowitz's story of Saturday classes at Harvard is reported by him in *Chutzpah*. Boston: Little, Brown, 1991, p. 64.

172. Disraeli's all-purpose line is attributed to him in several collections. Robert Andrews (*The Concise Columbia Dictionary of Quotations*, New York: Columbia University Press, 1990, p. 56) renders the line as part of a broader statement: "When I meet a man whose name I can't remember, I give myself two minutes, then if it is a hopeless case, I always say: 'And how is the old complaint?'" However no source is offered. I recall reading the line in a biography of Disraeli but skimming through a number of biographies has not been fruitful.

Clifton Fadiman's addition of the literary line is in Clifton Fadiman (ed.) *The Little, Brown Book of Anecdotes*, Boston: Little, Brown, p. 171.

173. The quotation from actor Ted Danson was from a TV show, 20/20 in 1990 as rendered in John Whitcomb and Claire Whitcomb, *Great American Anecdotes*, New York: William Morrow, 1993, p. 65.

173-174. Philip G. Zimbardo, *Shyness: What It is. What to Do About It*, Reading, MA: Addison-Wesley, 1977, p. 85.

174. "Refulgent respectability" is treated in Laud Humphreys, *Tearoom Trade*, Chicago: Aldine, 1970. See also Frederick J. Desroches, Tearoom Trade: A Research Update, *Qualitative Sociology*, 13, 1990, 39-61 .

The motel study is J. Robert Lilly and Richard A. Hall, "Challenges to Situated Morality: Maintaining Respectability in a Sexual Rendezvous," *Qualitative Sociology*. 3, 1980, 204-221.

Robert B. Cialdini and Kenneth D. Richardson, "Two Tactics of Image Management: Basking and Blasting,"*Journal of Personality and Social Psychology*, 39, 1980, 406-415. A summary piece by the same authors is in James T. Tedeschi (ed.) *Impression Management Theory and Social Psychological Research*, New York: Academic Press, 1981, Chap. 3.

175. David S. Davis, "Good People Doing Dirty Work: A Study of Social Isolation," *Symbolic Interaction*, 7, 1984, 233-247. The quotation is on p. 241.

175. Raymond Gold, "Janitors vs. Tenants: A Status-Income Dilemma," In Arnold Birenbaum amd Edward Sagarin (eds.) *People in Places*, New York: Praeger, 1973, pp. 257-268. The original article was published in 1952.

177-178. The problem of being too good looking may be related to being over-praised as discussed in Arnold H. Buss, *Self-Consciousness and Social Anxiety*, San Francisco, W. H. Freeman and Co., 1980, pp. 138-140. Overpraise is interpreted as causing secret feelings of really being superior which are felt to be immodest. Hence the embarrassment.

180. Carol Brooks Gardner's studies include "Passing By: Street Remarks, Address Rights and the Urban Female," *Sociological Inquiry*, 5, 1980, 328-356; "Access Information: Public Life and Private Peril," *Social Problems*,

35, 1988, 384-397; "Analyzing Gender in Public Places: Rethinking Goffman's Vision of Everyday Life," *The American Sociologist*, Spring, 1989, 42-56. The latter reference includes the quotation of the man offering to remove the woman's dress, p. 51. "Safe Conduct: Women, Crime and Self in Public Places," *Social Problems*, 37, 1990, 311-328.

181. The European study was reported in *Ms Magazine*, May, 1981, pp. 18-19 under the title: "The Man in the Street: Why He Hassles."

182. Lindsay van Gelder's report and advice appeared in *Ms Magazine*, May, 1981, p. 17.

CHAPTER 11: SOCIAL MOVES

185-186. Good technical discussions of altercasting can be found in Eugene Weinstein and Paul Deutschberger, "Some Dimensions of Altercasting," *Sociometry*, 26, 1963, 454-466 and by the same authors, "Tasks, Bargains and Identities in Social Interaction," *Social Forces*, 42, 1964, 451-456. A later study is reported in Philip W. Blumstein, "Audience, Machiavelianism and Tactics of Identity Bargaining," *Sociometry*, 36, 1973, 346-365.

187. Michael Holroyd's problem with a member of the British royal family is from Robert Morley, *Book of Bricks*, New York: G. P. Putnam's Sons, 1979, p. 23.

188. Bert R. Brown and Howard Garland, "The Effects of Incompetency, Audience Acquaintanceship and Anticipated Evaluative Feedback on Face-Saving Behavior," *Journal of Experimental Social Psychology*, 7, 1971, 490-502.

Robert J. Edelmann and Sarah E. Hampson, "Changes in Non-verbal Behaviour During Embarrassment," *British Journal of Social and Clinical Psychology*, 18, 1979, 385-390, and "The Recognition of Embarrassment," *Personality and Social Psychology Bulletin*, 7, 1981, 109-116.

189. The discussion of the elements of an apology is in Erving Goffman, *Relations in Public*, New York: Harper and Row, 1971, p. 113.

195. Harold Garfinkel's experiments on upsetting everyday expectations in department stores are described in Harold Garfinkel, *Studies in Ethnomethodology*, Englewood Cliffs, NJ: Prentice-Hall, 1967 .

195-196. Schnorrers are described in the article "Folklore" in the *Encyclopedia Judaica*, Vol. 6. A good sociological study of modern-day schnorrers in a Jewish Orthodox congregation is Samuel C. Heilman, "The Gift of Alms," *Urban Life and Culture*, 3, 1975, 371-395. Brief treatments can be found in Leo Rosten's works: *The Joys of Yiddish*, New York: McGraw Hill, 1968, pp. 360-362 and *Hooray For Yiddish*, New York: Simon and Schuster, 1982, pp. 302-304.

198. James P. Curran and Peter M. Monti, *Social Skills Training: A Practical Handbook for Assessment and Treatment*, New York: Guilford, 1982. Also worth consulting is Michael Argyle, *Social Skills and Work*, New York: Methuen, 1981 .

CHAPTER 12: ENJOYING EMBARRASSMENT

203. The incident of the woman who decided to copy her backside happened in Moline, Illinois as reported in the *Seattle Times*, Feb. 27, 1980.

203-204. Thomas J. Scheff, "Control Over Policy by Attendants in a Mental Hospital," *Journal of Health and Social Behavior*, 2, 1961, 93-105.

204-205. Marcia Millman, *The Unkindest Cut*, New York: William Morrow, 1977, Chap. 8.

205. George A. Test, "The Roast: American Ritual Satire and Humor," in Ray B. Browne (ed.), *Rituals and Ceremonies in Popular Culture*, Bowling Green: Bowling Green University Popular Press, 1980.

"power and prominence...humor." From George A. Test, "The Roast," cited above, p. 166.

206. The roast of Senator Throm Thurmond was reported in the *New York Times*, Sept. 24, 1982.

The story of John F. Kennedy's retort before the Gridiron Club is from Theodore C. Sorensen, *Kennedy*, New York: Harper and Row, 1965, p. 119.

207. President Taft's quotation is from George A. Test, "The Roast," cited above, p. 171.

Chauncey Depew's statement of the goal of the club is quoted in the George A. Test study cited above, p. 172.

Of course poking holes in pretension is not the only reason persons may deliberately embarrass others. Professor of Speech Willam F. Sharkey analyzed reports of intentional embarrassment from 1136 persons ranging in age from 18 to 77. He found the most common to be some form of recognition or praise such as giving someone a retirement party. Sharkey found such occasions to betoken a goal of showing solidarity. William F. Sharkey, "Intentional Embarrassment: Goals, Tactics and Consequences," in William R. Cupach & Sandra Metts (eds.) *Advances in Interpersonal Communication Research*, Proceedings of the Western States Communication Association, Interpersonal Communication Group, 1991, pp. 106-128.

209. Enid Welsford, *The Fool: His Social and Literary History*, London: Faber and Faber, 1935. The quotation is from p. xi.

210. Leo Rosten's stories of the irrepressible Hyman Kaplan are in *O K*A*P*L*A*N, My K*A*P*L*A*N*, New York: Harper and Row, 1976.

210-211. Stephen Pile, *The Incomplete Book of Failures*, New York: Dutton, 1979. The lost explorer's exploits are on p. 3. The barge theft attempt is on p. 62.

211. Saul Bellow's statement I have from Ruth R. Wisse's study, *The Schlemiel as Modern Hero*, Chicago: University of Chicago Press, 1971, p. 101.

212. Robert Louis Stevenson's saying on failing in good spirits is on p. 1 of the Stephen Pile collection cited above. After diligent search, I am unable to find any source for the saying, but it seems most apposite.

213. The Fritz Perls quotation is from Carl D. Schneider, *Shame, Exposure and Privacy*, Boston: Beacon Press, 1977, p. xiv.

214. Christopher Ricks, *Keats and Embarrassment*, London: Oxford University Press, 1974. The quotation is on pp. 50-51. According to Ricks, the poet Keats seems to have been almost perpetually bothered by embarrassment.

Gun R. Semin and A.S. R. Manstead, "The Social Implications of Embarrassment Displays and Restitution Behaviour," *European Journal of Social Psychology*, 12, 1982, 367-377.

215. The study showing that flubs by superior persons are especialy likely to make that person seem attractive is Elliot Aronson, Ben Willerman and Joanne Floyd, "The Effect of a Pratfall on Increasing Interpersonal Attractiveness," *Psychonomic Science*, 4, 1966, 227-228. A later study taking into account the position of the observer and the role of self-esteem is Robert Helmreich, Elliot Aronson and James LeFan, "To Err is Humanizing—Sometimes," *Journal of Personality and Social Psychology*, 16, 1970, 259-264.

Singer Richard Harris' experience with lyrics to the song in *Camelot* is reported in the *Seattle Post-Intelligencer*, Jan. 27,1983.

INDEX

To avoid unnecessary duplication of personal names, only names which appear in the text or new citations added to REFERENCES AND COMMENTS are included below.

246

247

248